What People Are Saying About Journey

Journey is one of the best words I can think of to describe our life-long, ever-winding, ever adventuress walk with Christ. In this book, my friend, Glenn Sauls, does an amazing job of unpacking the faith stirring stories of the Bible and relating them to the personal story God has for each one of us. Reading the book will position you in a place to clearly see God's vision for your life. Glenn has personally been an encouragement to me, and throughout *Journey,* you too will be encouraged as you discover God's amazing purpose for your life. **- Jeff Little, Lead Pastor, Milestone Church in Keller, TX**

Journey is a great reminder that the Creator God, made you and me, with a "you" specific plan in mind. In this book, my friend, Dr. Glenn Sauls, helps you realize not only who you are, but how God has uniquely gifted you for your specific life journey. It's through great spiritual and practical insight that Glenn leads you into a journey to discover your God-given purpose. **- Dino Rizzo, Lead Pastor, Healing Place Church in Baton Rouge, LA**

My good friend, Glenn, has hit a home run with his book, *Journey.* Christians have been told for years that they should link their lives to the spiritual journey God has designed for them. The problem is, no one has ever talked about what that spiritual journey looks like. Dr. Sauls has put together a roadmap for success as you move toward being everything God has made you to be and called you to be. I recommend *Journey* to anyone who is serious about growing in their spiritual life and achieving great things for God! **- Bryan Carter, Senior Pastor, Concord Church in Dallas, TX**

This book by my friend, Dr. Sauls, is a "must read" for all Christians from the standpoint that it truly motivates all of us off the sidelines of life and into the game that God has uniquely designed for us.

Glenn is a great spiritual coach, and *Journey* will get you in the game spiritually. I recommend this book to anyone who wants to achieve in life at a high level and thrive in their God-given sweet-spot. - **Bishop Claude Alexander, Senior Pastor, The Park Church in Charlotte, NC**

Dr. Glenn Sauls helps bring clear focus for the dream to build up people in Christ. His carefully constructed words of wisdom drip with purpose and meaning to see even greater things occur in the lives of believers. Glenn's voice in my life has provided an appreciation to leave a legacy that others can come under and then carry to new heights. I hope you will pick up this great read and take to heart Glenn's teaching. - **Erik Lawson, Lead Pastor, Element Church in Wentzville, MO**

JOURNEY:

WHERE ARE YOU GOING TODAY?

by

Glenn Sauls

Romans 8:28

To Sister Wanda,

My prayer is that as you read Journey, you will move forward in pursuing God's "best" for your life. Don't ever settle for good, go for God's best.

Blessings,

ISBN: 978-1-936750-65-8

Dedicated by my Parents Charlie and Joann Sauls

For all their years of modeling Christianity for me

And

My Sons, David and Jonathan

The Greatest Sons A Dad Could Ever Have

And

My Grandma

For the incredible Christian heritage she has given to me and all our family

Foreword by Steve Robinson

Senior Pastor, Church of the King
Mandeville, LA

For much of my adult Christian life, I have either heard the term or used the term, *spiritual journey.* People talk about it, muse about it, discuss it, pray about it, but few have ever taken time to define what the spiritual journey for a devoted follower of Christ truly looks like. As any journey, there are so many defining moments in the spiritual journey. Also, the spiritual journey for Christians is as unique as each individual.

In Journey, Dr. Glenn Sauls has found some major mile markers that can be seen in the life of every person. While the journey is truly unique for each individual, there are some things we see in God's Word that tend to mark the path of every follower of Christ. Glenn has taken those rare markers that appear across the board in every believer and has put them into a book that is informative, exciting, filled with great stories, and prioritized so that everyone can truly get it.

These truths have not just remained in the "Sauls laboratory," but they have been tested in churches of all different sizes, denominations, ethnicities, and styles across America. This book actually started out as a devotional guide for churches. Then, Glenn added sermons and small group lessons that have been truly field tested. This book is the result of four years of churches using these thoughts and seeing incredible spiritual and financial impact.

Glenn has been a dear friend of mine for nearly ten years and has worked closely with Church of the King on a consultant basis. I have watched Glenn lead. He has led alongside of me. I have watched him in meetings with my key staff members and seen how God has used him to bring clarity at key crossroads in the life of our church. God has given Glenn the ability to work with churches and bring an anointing that often goes beyond just his consulting role.

The truths you will find in Journey were not born in some office or think tank. These thoughts were birth in the heart and soul of a real guy, a leader, that truly loves the local church, its people, and the mission and vision of what God has called churches to do and be. Glenn has been in the trenches. He knows what it is like to pastor. He knows what it is like to come alongside pastors across America and consult and coach.

You will be encouraged by Glenn's thoughts, his hopes for you, and the clarity of his writing style. Join me on this journey and watch as God brings incredible crossroads to your life. And when they come, you will truly be glad you were prepared for those moments by reading Journey.

- Mandeville, LA 2011

Introduction

As I prepared to write this book on the subject of what a spiritual journey looks like for the Christian, I discovered there are a lot of books on the market concerning "a spiritual journey." I further discovered that most of the writing is not from the evangelical Christian perspective. Much of it was from a Zen, Buddhist, and Christian Science take on what a spiritual journey may be. For years, as a church consultant, I have heard the spiritual journey talked about in various shapes and forms. I have talked to church pastors and leaders about "linking their congregants to the spiritual journey" or, "connecting everyone to a spiritual journey as opposed to a financial journey." We say things like that because my company partners with churches and pastors across America to provide coaching and resources for doing capital stewardship campaigns.

Raising finances in the local church, particularly involving sacrificial or special project dollars, is about connecting people to a spiritual journey, in hopes that the congregants will respond with passion for the vision of the church and give "over and above" for whatever the project or ministry initiative being advanced at the time. It is our belief at Sauls Consulting Services that if we present the need in a way that is reflective of what is pleasing to God and do it in a compelling and catalytic manner, the people of God always feel honored to support what God is doing through their church.

We see this illustrated in scripture in 1 Chronicles 29:5 and 6, when David stands before the leadership of Israel and asked them a simple, yet deeply spiritual, question, *"Now, who is willing to consecrate himself today to the Lord."* I don't think anyone reading this would deny that this is a spiritual question, not a financial question. Yet, the leaders of Israel responded financially, *"Then the leaders...gave willingly."* David led by connecting the people of Israel to a spiritual journey that moved them to respond to the project by giving willingly.

But even in this story, we find that God put the dream for this project, building the Temple of God, into a man's heart. Great dreams start in the heart of God and He then puts it in a man's or woman's heart to be carried out on earth. In the beginning of this story, David makes a statement that brings such clarity to this thought. He says in 1 Chronicles 28:2, *"I had it in my heart to build a house as a place of rest for the ark of the covenant of the Lord...."* The dream of having a permanent place to mark the presence of God began in the leader's heart. God put a dream in David's heart and it started him on a journey to see God's plan come to fruition. It truly was a compelling vision that became the catalyst for passion and action in the lives of the people of God.

The dream typically goes from the heart of the leader to being shaped into a vision that can be cast as a roadmap for the journey. The shaping of the vision usually includes the fact that on this journey, God has to show up. If you can accomplish your dream without God, then your dream is too small. In 1 Chronicles 29:1, David says, *"The task is great, because this palatial structure is not for man but for the Lord God."* In other words, the vision that God has called me to is big; it is bigger than I am, and if God doesn't show up, I'm in the tank. God's dream for your life is big. You will need God's help to be successful on this journey that He has prepared for you.

The journey God has called you to will also demand sacrifice at times on your part. In this same story, David talks about the sacrifice He is willing to make for the dream. In verse three, he says, *"Besides, in my devotion to the temple of my God I now give my personal treasures of gold and silver for the temple of my God, over and above everything I have provided for this holy temple..."* (1 Chronicles 29:3). There will be times in your life that accomplishing God's dream for your life will demand occasional and/or seasonal "over and above" living. There may be occasions when opportunities come and you will be asked to give more than you are already giving. God will stretch you into faith territory to see if you will truly trust Him. "Over and above" living says that we are not going to "play it safe" when it comes to our journey of faith. If God can get a miracle to me, He can get it through me. I am willing to step out in faith territory and believe God will use me to advance His dream in my life.

I came to a point in my faith journey in the late 1990s that I knew I would have to trust God in a new way. The church I was pastoring was in a capital stewardship campaign and as a family, we were praying about what we were going to give "over and above" our tithes and offerings. We came to a decision that God was speaking to us about giving up my retirement to see God's dream for our church advanced. We heard God's voice speak and we were obedient to doing what He was challenging us to do. It was no small thing to us. God was taking us into faith territory. I tell people all the time that nobody takes care of old pastors. They put old pastors out to pasture.

We decided not to "play it safe" and live in faith territory. There will be seasons in your life that God will call you to "over and above" living. By the way, it is a season and most people only face this season two or three times in their lives. It is important that you are walking this journey out in faith so when the opportunity comes, you are in a position to respond by faith. I call these "crossroads of opportunities." These crossroads are times in your life when God presents an opportunity to you to move His Kingdom forward exponentially by responding in faith. These are catalytic moments that the Kingdom moves forward and nobody can take earthly credit for what has happened. We all stand back and say, "God must have done that!" The problem for a lot of people is they have not lived their lives in such a way to be in a position when the opportunity comes to truly accept it and watch God do a miracle through them.

If God wanted to use you as a catalyst for His Kingdom, are you living your life in a way that you are in a position to respond by faith? Are you, right now, in a position that God can use you? I was sitting on an airplane in the early 90s and the man sitting beside me started talking to me about an idea his company had for a "virtual mall" that would be on something called the internet. I had no idea what he was talking about at that time. He was giving me the opportunity to invest early and be a part of something people would start doing later that we now know as "shopping on the internet." And, almost everyone does it. The problem for me was I wasn't in a financial position to take a risk on his company's dream. I don't know, but he could have been the guy that started the whole "shopping on line" trend. I lost his card and cannot remember his name.

The point is, simply, I was not in a position to take advantage of a "crossroads" moment in my life. I wanted to be an early adopter, but I was not in a position to take advantage of this "crossroad opportunity." God wants us to live the journey in a way that we are positioned for those "crossroads" moments when God intervenes in our lives.

I have heard this spiritual journey talked about most of the thirty-three years I have spent in ministry. The first twenty-two years I spent in the local church. The last eleven, I have served local churches across America as a church consultant. God has allowed me to live out His calling in my life by partnering with pastors and churches to see them achieve maximum impact in their communities by assisting them to be all that God has made them to be.

In this book called *Journey*, my dream is to help you discover the unique journey God has laid out for you in this life. While every single person's journey is unique, there are some reoccurring mile markers that I have seen over the years that will help you stay on course and maximize your impact in this world for Christ.

I have found those non-negotiable mile markers in everyone's life to be these five things:

1. Discovering, developing, and living out God's vision for your life.
2. Living a fully stewarded life to Jesus Christ by keeping everything that God has given to you fully surrendered on the altar of sacrifice.
3. Once everything is on the altar and you understand that God owns it all and you are just the manager, listen for God's voice in your life. I have discovered that God just cannot be limited to communicating the way we think He should communicate. We serve a "creative" God and He is always speaking to us in new and creative ways.
4. After you have been able to distinguish God's voice speaking to you, be obedient to what He is saying. There is a huge chasm that often exists between hearing God's voice and implementing what He is saying to you in your life.
5. Once you have come to the place where you have surrendered everything to God and you are listening attentively to His voice, you are being obedient to His voice; then, leave room for God's miraculous intervention in your life. God will bring God-designed crossroads into your life from time to time. It is your responsibility to be in a spiritual place that you can respond to His intervention in faith and service.

Everyone's journey is different and will be splashed with all kinds of unique "colors" from God along the way. It would be impossible for me to outline your life journey, but I do think I can help you recognize some key mile markers that you should be seeing along the way. If you are not seeing them, it may mean you have temporarily veered off the path that God has designed and prepared for you in this life.

So, how do we stay on the path that God has prepared for us? And by the way, God does prepare a journey for every single one of His children and it is our responsibility to embrace that path and prepare ourselves for our journey. The sin of comparison often keeps people in the church from embracing their path wholeheartedly. “Well, if I could teach like Jim, then I would speak all the time.” Or, “If I could sing like (you fill in the blank), then I would be on the worship team every Sunday.” It is the “if and then” syndrome that knocks people off the journey that God has uniquely laid out for them. Why is it that someone else’s journey can look so much better than the one God designed for us? With the carefully planned out gifts, passions, talents, abilities, personalities, and life experiences that God has given to us, why would we think we fit someone else’s journey better than our own?

To truly enjoy the spiritual journey, we have to be content with and fully embrace the life that God has designed for us. Get happy! Be the person God has made you to be. Nobody else can be you and no one else can accomplish the things God has laid out for you to do in this life. I don’t get it all, either. Sometimes, I wish God would let me have Bill Gate’s journey, or Donald Trump’s. It just seems that a lot of money makes the journey smoother and more enjoyable. I cannot answer that one but I do believe that fulfillment comes from embracing God’s dream for your life and making it happen.

Recently, I was spending time with a friend who has had much success in the music industry. She started out singing in church and over the years, she has had hit records in the R&B /Hip Hop world. She has performed on stage and recordings with some of the most renowned music stars in America. After all, she performed on Oprah! She has performed in front of thousands of people all over the world and now, she is at a different place in her life. What has impressed me about her is she still works on her craft. She is singularly focused on being the very best singer she can be. She may have gotten tired along the way in her journey, but she continues to fully embrace what it is and never wishes she had someone else's music career. She has caught a vision of what it is that God has made her to be and she fully embraces it and lives it out with zest every single day.

Embracing God's Vision For Your Journey

In my travels with Sauls Consulting, I often find myself in new cities trying to find the location of a new church/client. Before I leave the office and get on a plane, I google or map the location of the church from the airport. On most of the maps, I see things like, "If you get to Maple Street, you have gone past your turn." Not only do they give you turn-by-turn directions, but they also give you mile markers in case you get off the path of your location. Having a clear vision for your life not only let's you know where you are going, but it allows you to know if you have taken a wrong turn and gotten off the path that God has laid out for you.

Writing out a mission/vision statement for your life will not take long. It needs to be simple. It is not a document that you will be using to impress others. This vision statement is for you! It should be clear, concise, compelling, catalytic, and contextual. You should reduce it down to three to five statements about your journey in life that you can memorize and own.

The vision statement should have clarity and it should bring clarity to everything you attempt to do in life. It is your statement that you hold up against every new adventure that comes your way. It helps you to say "Yes" to the right thing and "No" to the wrong thing. By the way, sometimes the most spiritual thing you can do in your life journey is to say "No." Not every good thing that comes along is right for you. I have often heard it said that "Good is the enemy of the best." God has the best for you in your journey, so quit settling for good. Settling for good can make you happy in the moment, so don't misunderstand me. But the "best" will bring long-term fulfillment to your life. It will be the thing that wakes you up with excitement in the morning and lays you down with peace and contentment at night.

As I mentioned earlier, the statement should be concise. Make it memorable and repeatable. If you don't get it, it will never work for you. I remember when I was pastoring in North Carolina, our leadership team decided to develop a vision statement for our church. Now, this was back in the early 90s when it was just beginning to be popular to have a church vision statement. Now, everyone has one, whether they can remember where they put it or not. We went away on a leadership retreat and designed a statement that ended up thirteen pages long. Needless to say, we had an impressive document, though nobody owned it. Your life vision statement should be usable, so make it concise. It truly can be a compass for you as you travel this journey called life.

The statement should also be compelling in nature. God has created you for great exploits; thus, your vision statement should reflect that thought. I was sitting at a conference in 1990 at Willow Creek Community Church. On this particular afternoon, Jim Collins was being interviewed by Bill Hybels. This is the same Jim Collins that wrote the great business books, *Good to Great* and *Built to Last*. During his interview conversation with Hybels, he made a statement that truly influenced my life. His words were something like this: "If you were no longer on the face of this earth, what would the people around you miss?" In other words, if you no longer existed, would it matter? What would those who are in your life miss? Why don't you try answering that question; it will give you a pretty good idea why God put you here. It will give you a great start by just bullet pointing out some thoughts on what would your circle of influence miss if all of a sudden you were gone.

Take those thoughts and begin to write out a vision statement that is clear, concise, compelling, and catalytic. The statement should bring such clarity and purpose to your life that it should catapult you into new effectiveness and laser-like attention. To be catalytic means that it will move you forward on your journey exponentially as though you were in a Ferrari, instead of riding a bicycle.

Last, your life vision statement should be contextualized for you personally. It should reflect the gifts, passions, abilities, talents, and life experiences God has brought into your life. This allows you to see clearly how God has equipped you for the journey he has called you for in life. Your statement should reflect your uniqueness, which keeps you from falling into the comparison thing. When I was pastoring, it was not unusual to have a young person come to me and talk about God's dream for his or her life. Inevitably, the conversation would get around to what I called the "fear factor." Many of them were afraid that God would send them to Africa as a missionary, or keep them poor and humble, or serving the hurting in India. What they did not understand is if God calls you to those kinds of ministries, He will give you a heart for it. As the old saying goes, "What God has called you to do, He has equipped you to do."

God will put it in your heart. What do you think it means when the Psalmist says, "God will give you the desires of your heart"? Did you think it meant He will give you any little ol' thing you want? The Psalmist is saying, God will put the right desires in your heart. He will give you a heart for what He has called you to do. He will give such a passion for Africa, or the hurting of those in India, that you will feel empty unless you are serving in those areas.

You can quit resisting God's call on your life. Open your heart to what He is saying to you through His Word and the Holy Spirit. God wants you to be fulfilled more than you want it. God does not desire to put "round pegs in square holes." His specialty is putting you in the place He has uniquely prepared you to be. He prepares you for your life task by giving you all the tools to be successful.

As you own your vision statement, it will continue to keep you saying yes to the right things and no to the wrong things. At times, you will drift from the original statement you have written. By referring back to the vision for your life, it keeps you from dilution and unintentionally altering what God has called you to be. It does not happen overnight. There will be times when you will simply drift from your mission, and it is in those times that you look back at your original vision statement and return to the journey God has created for you. You will find that you must remain vigilant and pay attention to the vision mile markers in your life. It is so easy to chase after someone else's dream and find yourself way off course.

Vision, on its own, will fade over time. If it were easy to live your life by a vision statement, everyone would be doing it. In fact, this is what sets highly successful and fulfilled people apart from those that fall for anything that comes along. You just cannot push autopilot and expect to stay on the journey. Typically, the expectations of others will pull you off the path, either to the left or right. You will need to keep your vision statement firmly in front of you and even then, some drift will happen. You will continually need to recalibrate and make course corrections as you move forward in your spiritual journey.

Andy Stanley often talks about vision as what should be and could be, but will not be if we do not remain focused on the journey. It is so easy for the moment or the urgent to overwhelm the vision for the journey. The moment can simply be the paying of bills, cleaning the gutters, or washing the family's clothes. All these things are important but they can temporarily cause vision to fade. The urgent can be braces for the kids, a car accident, putting a parent in a care facility; big things in life that can overwhelm us and cause us to lose focus on our existence.

Having a clear vision for your life gives you the infrastructure for organizing your life. Although it is difficult to stay on task, having a vision for your life will give you a point to keep coming back to over time. So, what does the preferred future look like for you? Have you written that vision statement that keeps you on track in life's journey? It is the first and most important mile marker for you to identify in your journey. I hope you will stop reading for a while and just give some honest and uninterrupted thought to what God's preferred dream for your life looks like.

As you move through the journey, living out the vision for your life will bring credibility to what you say about yourself. People will want to be around you and they will want to follow you. Establishing yourself as a person driven by vision will make others want to line up behind you. They will see that you are driven by purpose and not by the latest whim that comes over the television or internet. As one person once said, "If you don't stand for something, you will fall for anything." Having vision will give you the courage to truly believe in what you are doing with your life. It will give you the strength to carry it out with purpose. Others will see how you boldly live your life and it will encourage them to do the same.

Vision lays out the roadmap for your life and allows you to finish your journey at a predetermined place with respect and dignity. That sounds really good, doesn't it? All of us want to finish our journey well. At the end of life, we all want to hear those famous words from scripture, "Well done, good and faithful servant." To finish well, you have to plan well. Believe me, you never have to recover from a good start. Most people spend their whole lives trying to find God's will. They are looking for the path God has designed for them. It is better to start early than late, but the best time to start is now. Don't make excuses. It is never too late to write out your personal vision statement. You have to embrace who God has made you to be and live out the vision He has placed in your heart.

Once again, to do that, I believe you have to write it down. I think of the words in Habakkuk 2:2, *"Write down the revelation and make it plain on tablets...."* Write it down so you can come back to it for regular course corrections. Keep it simple. Don't try to impress others. This document is for you. Make it memorable. You cannot retain paragraphs, so try putting it into three to five bullet points. It is not of very much value to you if it not memorable.

Oh, and by the way, celebrate the little "wins" in the spiritual journey. We tend to do what is celebrated. When you make a hard decision based on your vision for the journey, do something to celebrate it and mark that moment. Those memories will keep you on the journey and help to remind you why you do what you do in this life. I have found in my own journey that what gets celebrated gets done. If you truly want to stay in the game and stay focused on your journey, take the time to mark a "win" with something significant.

Living your life's journey based on the vision God has given to you will cost you at times. Sometimes it will cost you convenience or popularity. It may cost you business or a significant relationship. Embrace the vision that God has given to you. It is truly the key mile marker in your life's journey.

Once you have established a vision for your life, there are four other mile markers that will also keep you on the path to fulfill the journey God has called you to in this life. Over the next four sections of *Journey*, stay with me as we look at these major mile markers in your life. You will be able to see these markers and then begin to personalize them in your life. Nothing becomes dynamic until it becomes personal in your life.

These mile markers in the journey are general mapping points for anyone who will choose to follow Christ. However, they will lead you to decisions that will become very personal in your life:

> Choosing to settle the issue of ownership in your life is important. How you will settle it is personal and practical.
>
> Choosing to listen to the voice of God in your life is important. How God speaks to you is personal and practical.

Choosing to be obedient to what God says to you is important. How you walk out obedience in your life is personal and practical.

Choosing to allow God to intervene in your life is important. How God miraculously intervenes in your life is personal and practical.

The journey is exciting and waiting to be explored, so let's get started and see what God does in your life!

Section 1

But...What If I Surrendered Everything? Scary!

"The world has yet to see what God will do with and through and in and by the man who is fully consecrated to Him."

- Dwight L. Moody

A Double Test

In early 2000 while still pastoring in North Carolina, our church went on a missions outreach in Baguio City, Philippines. A former staff member of mine and his family were now serving as missionaries to this area of Asia. I had taken a group of about fifty people from our church and one of the projects was building a new church at Camp Six, which is just outside of Baguio.

For me, I was speaking at a denominational seminary and teaching about a hundred national pastors daily on how to use spiritual gifts to grow their church. This was a great time and opportunity for me. I loved speaking to these pastors and equipping them to grow their churches. Everyday was filled with new challenges. One of those challenges was helping these pastors who spoke English as a second or third language, to understand this southern pastor who, as someone said, "spoke American, not English!" Nevertheless, it was exciting to watch them as they began to understand how God had equipped the church with gifted people whose passions, abilities, personalities, and experiences could be used to advance God's Kingdom.

The other reason it was so exciting for me personally was the fact that my oldest son, David, twelve years old at the time,2 was with me on this adventure. Everyday, he would work with the rest of the team from our church to build a place of worship for those living in the Camp Six area. He was a natural. He fit right in with the team, and more importantly, with the children from the area. They fell in love with him and he fell in love with the people of Camp Six. The team would spend time daily doing outreach to the neighboring area and David was right there playing ball and having all kinds of fun with the local children. It was so cool and unnerving watching my little twelve-year-old run across a little wooden and rope bridge, forty feet above a river, with a bag of cement on his shoulder. His mother would have fainted on the spot!

Little did I know at the time, that this was the beginning of a "double test" in my life.

Have you ever wondered what would happen if you truly surrendered everything to God? That's a scary thought for most of us—at least, if we are honest. Has the thought ever crossed your mind that if I surrender everything to God, He will make me poor and homeless, or He will make me go to Africa as a missionary, or He will make me move to some remote part of America, or worse, the world, and serve Him in obscurity?

Sure, you have! Most honest Christians would confess that the thought has crossed their minds in a somewhat vulnerable moment. When I was pastoring, I can remember several occasions on Sunday mornings as I stood before the people I served, and said, "God is more interested in your character than your comfort. I don't like that at all. I like comfort." Just trying to be truthful and vulnerable.

Yet, isn't it true that God desires that we enjoy and experience life at its fullest? In fact, He has said that in the Bible (John 10:10). So, how do we obtain this "life to the full" that Jesus talks about in the book of John? There are probably a lot of good answers to that question that can be given by people that understand the Bible at a much deeper level than me.

But, if you would allow me, I would like to suggest that we go on a spiritual journey that could give us some answers to how we could live a revolutionary life filled with absolute fullness and fulfillment–not to mention, incredible grace and peace!

Along the journey, we will see that quite often, we will face significant tests that are not meant to discourage us but serve as catalysts in our relationship with God. I started the first grade in public school at the age of five and I have been in schools and colleges most of my life. I have learned a few things about tests and examinations over the last forty or fifty years. I have come to a non-scientific conclusion that nobody gives an examination like God. He will thoroughly prepare you, if allowed to, and He will thoroughly examine you, as well.

I am sure you understand what I'm saying and I'm sure you would agree that an untested and unexamined life is one that will underachieve at what God has called someone to do and shaped him or her to be. So how do we "get good" at this journey that is littered with tests and examinations? And—why are we being tested? One more thing: When do we know we have passed and gone to the head of the class? Good questions!

A life lived to the fullest and filled with fulfillment is more about the journey than some destination that God has set out there in our future. The roadmap is certainly important so let me lay out for you a few mile markers that will help to keep us on the spiritual journey that God has uniquely designed for each of us. By the way, your journey will not look like mine, but I do believe the mile markers will look the same.

This spiritual journey moves us from where we are, which typically is marked by the question, "What am I going to do with my life for God?" Not a bad question, but I believe there is a better question that we are continually moving toward in this spiritual journey, called "Full Life." That question is, "God, what do You want to do through my life on this earth?" You see, it is not about my best efforts, but it is more about God's hand working in and through my life.

Chapter 1

Re-Surrender To Living God's Way

"Therefore, I urge you, brothers, in view of God's mercy, to offer your bodies as living sacrifices, holy and pleasing to God—this is your spiritual act of worship. Do not conform any longer to the pattern of this world, but be transformed by the renewing of your mind. Then you will be able to test and approve what God's will is—his good, pleasing and perfect will." Romans 12:1-2

As a pastor for many years, I cannot tell you how many times I had someone come to me and say, "Pastor, I just want to know what God's will is for my life," as if God was trying to hide His will from them. God wants you to know His will for your life more than you do. He is not playing "hide and seek" with His will. Sometimes, we just start in the wrong place. Most of God's will for your life is in His book called the Bible. It truly contains the revealed will of God for your life. Now, I know you are thinking, "But it's just not specific enough." You know what? You're right. However, the Bible contains the guidelines and mile markers for making every decision we will ever make in this life.

Here's where it all starts though. To understand God's good, pleasing, and perfect will, we must be willing to offer ourselves as "living sacrifices." It is an act of worship that serves as a direct catalyst toward understanding God's will—revealed and unrevealed—for our daily lives.

Some years ago, I heard the story of a man who had surgery on his right hand. He was in quite a bit of pain and his fingers were completely curled into a fist. It looked as though he was gripping something desperately in his hand. The doctor went in along his wrist and did some work and when he finished, the hand immediately opened. Where his hand was once "gripped" closed, it now was completely open and normal.

Sometimes, God has to go in and do surgery on our lives. We live with our lives proverbially closed and gripping everything we have like there is no tomorrow. It is not just a general surrender, or, as I like to say, "resurrender" of ourselves to God. That's too easy. It's too easy to stand in a worship service and sing I surrender all. Surrender doesn't get dynamic until it gets specific.

Now, let me explain what I mean by "resurrender." Isn't it true that at some point in your life, you surrendered everything to God? It's often called salvation or when you received Christ. Maybe it was at an altar, or in your car, or at your bedside. It could have been at some point of desperation in your life when you came to the conclusion that God's grace was intended for you. Or, it may have been like me just as a young child who trusted and accepted salvation. At some point, you declared you were a sinner and now you surrender your life to Christ. That means everything. All my possessions—money, family, children, career, education, savings- and your list could go on and on. But how often do we tend to go back to that altar where we surrendered everything to Him and take a thing or two off the altar? Maybe we think we can do better with our money or our kids or our job than God. So, not in a malicious way, but very quietly, we slip the "living sacrifice" off the altar.

What seems somewhat innocent in that moment is you saying to God, "I can handle this area of my life just fine. I can take it from here." You hold it with a clenched fist as though it somehow belongs to you. God says, "Alright, you're on your own. Wear yourself out."

So, there are those occasions in our lives when we have to come back to God and say, "Please take this off my plate. I'm not sleeping very well and it's sucking the life out of me." That is when the Holy Spirit does the surgery of clipping away until our hand relaxes and what we were holding with a clenched fist before God is now being held with an open hand. "God, it's all yours. Please take it back and I will manage it in a way that is pleasing to You." For so many people, it is their money. Or, at least, they think it's their money. Jesus understood that it would be difficult for us to live with an open hand when it comes to money. In fact, on one occasion he said, "You cannot serve God and money."

I started out telling you the story of my missions trip to Baguio. It was so interesting to watch my son in this ministry environment. David was such a natural. He blended in so well with the children. He worked hard, he played hard, and he ate whatever they ate. You don't really want to know what he ate. Let's just say sometimes it barks! He was so gifted and natural in the ministry environment. I truly believe God has his hand on David's life and has a unique calling in ministry for him. Our unique giftedness, talents, personalities, spiritual gifts, and experiences are usually a really good tip-off for the way God wants to use us in this life.

Now, I would prefer strongly that David never end up in a third world country somewhere half way around the world doing ministry. I want him to someday get married, live next door to me, and give me about three grandkids I can spoil and get back in him for what he did to me in his teenage years. That is called holding your children with a "clenched fist." "God, I have a better plan for David's life than You."

Is there some area of your life that has "crawled" off the altar of God? Not maliciously. Maybe you didn't even recognize it at the time. But now, as you look back over the last several years of your life, there are things that are now in your care of "ownership" that used to be in God's. So, what is it? Can you clearly and precisely identify it? Don't just do the 30,000 foot fly-over and say, "Well, everything is not on the altar." What is it that you are holding with a clenched fist? What is it that God is now saying to you, "You're on your own." Be specific. You will never feel the weight of it until you are specific with the area that you now control. So, what area or areas are you the boss of these days? Maybe it is your marriage, children, retirement, education, friendships, or relationships.

It is so important to take this survey of the "stuff" that God has entrusted to you. There is one thing I'm quite convinced of that will happen in the afterlife. One day, you will stand before God as someone who has received Christ, and He will ask you the BIG question, "What did you do with what I gave you?" In other words, He will ask you how you chose to use the possessions, gifts, talents, abilities, etc. that have been entrusted to you by God to faithfully steward in this life.

I think you would want to have a good answer to this one-question exam. Eye to eye, toe to toe, with the One who gave His life for you. Oh, and entrusted certain gifts, talents, abilities, etc. to you. Let's face it: We want to get this one right. "Oh, I took my money off the altar because I thought I had a better plan than You for my future and retirement." Doesn't sound too good as an answer, does it? Just say it out loud. It just doesn't feel right.

Re-surrender is not a one-time event. In fact, it is much more of a process along the spiritual journey. Why don't you take a moment right now and consider what it is in your life that may have crawled off the altar over time? Let's make sure we get this answer right!

Chapter 2

Where Are You In Control?

"But the Lord God called to the man, "Where are you?"
Genesis 3:9

Where are you? Where are you in control? What areas tend to land in your "ownership" category?

"Where are you?" It may not be the question you want to hear, but it is the question that God may be asking. It is a question that requires us to look at the "ownership" category of our lives. What is in our category and what is in God's? What is safely surrendered? What are we carrying on our own? This is uncomfortable and difficult because we have to take stock of ourselves and get truly honest with God.

"Where are you?' We don't want to deal with where we are. We prefer to take the 30,000 foot fly-over and suggest that most everything is on the altar. Or, we prefer to take a "hope so" strategy. Well, I hope everything is on the altar. Hope is not a strategy and it is not pleasing to God. We typically want to find a quick, pain-free escape out of the challenges and ownership issues that face us. Or, just flatly say, "It belongs to me. I did things the old fashion way. I earned it."

When Adam and Eve disobeyed God, what did they do? Well, it is what caused God to ask the question, "Where are you?" They were hiding. They had disobeyed God and hid from His presence.

The Lord wanted to give them His best, but they had rejected it. Yet, even in the midst of their disobedience and guilt, God wanted to show them the way back to fellowship with Him.

As you take inventory of your "ownership" category, it will be difficult at times. There will be things that you may consider trivial and think you can manage just fine by yourself. However, after some time, we tend to feel guilt for this attitude of ownership, and condemnation begins to set in. That condemnation will eventually alienate you from God. Think about it for a moment. Are there areas of ownership in your life that are beginning to steal "life to the fullest" from you?

It is important that we understand that guilt and condemnation always come from the devil. He is out to kill, steal, and destroy your "life to the fullest." That has always been his *M.O.* and it will never change. However, it is the Holy Spirit that comes to us and gently convicts and nudges us back to the spiritual journey that God has designed uniquely for us.

> *"For God did not send His Son into the world to condemn the world, but to save the world through Him."* John 3:17

"Where are you?" God asked the question to move Adam toward honesty about ownership in his life. So, where are you in the ownership category? This is a time to go through the tunnel of chaos and truly get honest with God.

I would like to think that my plan for my son's life is better than God's. However, I know who created him. I know that David is fearfully and wonderfully made in the image of God. He belongs to God, not me. Years ago, Ford Motor Company had a slogan that simply said, "Ford has a better idea!" Truthfully, as good as my ideas may be for my sons, God has a better idea! They are fearfully and wonderfully made in His image, and He knows what He has created them to do and be.

This truly is the stewardship question in our lives. If everything belongs to God, then what am I doing with it? *Am I managing it or am I controlling it?* What if you went through every major area of your life and asked the question, "Am I managing this or am I controlling it?" When it comes to my wealth, money, finances, retirement, and investments—am I managing and stewarding these areas of my life, or am I controlling them? Whose category of ownership do they fall into, God's or mine?

Am I controlling my marriage or is God in control? Am I controlling my relationships or is God in control? Am I controlling my career or is God in control? Am I controlling my children or is God in control of their lives?

Where are you?

You will never experience "life to the fullest" until you have decided ownership of all the areas of your life. By the way, I think this first step of declaring, "Who owns what" is very, very difficult. Sometimes, I wonder if we truly "get it" as followers of Christ. Sometimes, I wonder if I get it. Particularly in Western culture, which tends to be so materialistic, I think the issue of ownership is huge and very difficult for even the mature American Christian.

What is it truly like to say to God, "I am here, Lord. The ownership category of my life is wide open for you to inspect." In Luke 15, there is a story of a young man who ran away from home and his father. He had taken His inheritance and managed it quite poorly. I am sure he wasn't really ready to answer the question, "Where are you?" But, somewhere along the journey of life, the Bible says in Luke 15:17, he "came to his senses." He couldn't begin the journey back home to his father before he came to himself and did an inventory of who owns what in his life. But, there was a defining moment in his life when he realized where he was, with no plan of moving forward in a positive direction with his life.

The spiritual journey of a revolutionary life lived for God begins with answering the question, "Where are you?" Where am I when it comes to the possessions given to me by God? Who's in control of the possessions that God has entrusted to me? Am I managing all that God has given to me or am I controlling what God has invested in my life?

Keys To A Surrendered Life

There's a remarkable story in the Bible that is recorded in Genesis 22:1-18. It is the story of a man by the name of Abraham and how he responded when God asked him "Where are you?" In fact, his response was quite different from Adam's. He simply said to God, "Here I am."

God promised Abraham that he would be the father of many nations. In other words, Abraham was going to have a bunch of kids, grandkids, great grandkids! Well, you get it. There would be generations to follow Abraham. God had entrusted him with an incredible dream and mission that He would accomplish through Abraham's surrendered life. At the time that God dropped this vision for the world in Abraham's heart, he and Sarah had no children. Oh, that's not enough for you! Get this then: He was a hundred years old and his wife, Sara, was ninety years old when God finally gave him this promised son, Isaac. Think about it: The entire lineage of God's people rode on this promise.

It would have been easy for Abraham to just give up on the promise of God. It had been twenty-five years since God made the promise to him. Just as a personal observation, it seems the longer you have to wait for God to fulfill His dream in your life, the more significant the dream will be. Obviously, the birth of Isaac is going to be a pivotal event in the history of mankind. But, do not lose sight of the fact that it took tremendous faith in the life of Abraham to continue to believe for the promised son.

After the birth of Isaac and while he was still very young, Abraham was faced with another test of faith. God asked him to sacrifice this promised son to him on an altar of surrender. And get this: This wasn't just a spiritual altar, it was a real physical altar. God was asking Abraham to sacrifice his son to him. As this story goes, God was testing Abraham and once he passed the examination, God provided an alternate sacrifice in the form of a ram. As Abraham was getting prepared to take his son's life in sacrifice, God once again says to him, "Abraham, Abraham!" So he said, "Here I am."

When God asked Abraham "Where are you, what are you doing with what I gave you?" he was able to answer, "Here I am. What You have given to me belongs to you, I'm the manager but You, God, are the owner! Tell me what you want me to do with what you have given to me." In the next sentence of the story, God says to him, "Do not lay your hand on the lad, or do anything to him; for now I know that you fear God, since you have not withheld your son, your only son, from Me." Abraham passed the test of life. He aced the ownership test. In fact, he qualified for graduate school on this one.

What a powerful story of ownership. God owns it all, but He has incredibly entrusted me with some gifts, talents, abilities, possessions, and passions to steward in His honor. God asked Abraham if he would put that which he loved the most on the altar of sacrifice. In other words, would he hold Isaac with a clinched fist or an open hand?

For a moment, let's take a look at the antithesis. One of the richest men that ever owned anything was J. Paul Getty. On one occasion, someone asked him how much wealth would be enough for him. His answer was, "Just a little more." It is not that wealth is bad. God doesn't really care how much you own, as long as it doesn't own you. The opposite of generosity is hoarding. Just a little more. A little more than what? That's the problem. You are continually chasing an open-ended dream. I have a mental picture of Getty standing there with a clenched fist saying, "Just a little more."

How then do we keep the things we have surrendered on the altar and in the hands of God? Let's look at three key thoughts to managing your life in a God-honoring way:

1. Be willing to stay in a position of re-surrender. Just as God tested Abraham with his son, Isaac, He will test you with the things that are most important to you. My good friend and pastor, Steve Robinson, says it like this: "The more things you have that are important to you, the more you grow in life. The more successful you become, it is that much more of a test of re-surrendering all to God. Why? Because the more you have, the harder it is to risk it when God speaks."

The things that come off the altar quickest are the things we love the most. They tend to be the things that have the most possibility of possessing us. As Pastor Robinson says, "God is fine with us having possessions, with us having a great family, great dreams—as long as those things don't possess us." However, if we grip those things too tightly, they will get off the altar and hinder what God wants to do in our lives. As some would say, they become "idols" in our lives.

That is why God calls you and me to a life of re-surrender. That is the truth we saw in Romans 12 when Paul encourages us to continually offer up ourselves as living sacrifices to God. That's what we see in the life of Abraham. Abraham had already been asked by God to sacrifice significantly. He told him to move his family from their hometown and don't even ask where God is taking him. Abraham passed that test, as well. When it came time for the "ownership" test with Isaac, Abraham was willing. He lived his life as a continual process of re-surrender, not some one-time event.

2. Trust God that He will always provide for you. Re-surrendering requires that we have trust in God that He will provide for us in the midst of sacrifice and surrender. When Isaac asked his father, Abraham, where the sacrifice for the altar was, he simply said to him,

"My son, God will provide for Himself the lamb for a burnt offering." Abraham's experience with God in the past proved to him that God could be trusted with his future. What has been your experience with God in your past? In Genesis 22:14, it says, "Abraham called the name of the place, The-Lord-Will-Provide; as it is said to this day, "In the Mount of the Lord it shall be provided."

As I mentioned earlier, it was Abraham's experience with God in the past that built a foundation of trust for his future. He found that it was not an event, but rather it was a lifestyle of surrender. Twenty-five years of waiting and now God asks him to give Isaac up as a "living sacrifice." Abraham waited twenty-five years for the promise. Moses waited forty years to see God's vision for his life to become reality. Nehemiah waited four months to see the vision of a rebuilt Jerusalem. Yet, we often have a problem waiting four days, or four hours, to see God work and bring His vision for our lives to reality. Re-surrendering will take patience, perseverance, and trust in God at times. What is God doing between the time he sows a dream in our lives and bringing it to fruition? Well, I think there are at least three things going on: 1) He is maturing His dream in our heart and the maturation of a dream never happens without utter surrender; 2) God is growing us up spiritually and professionally to handle His dream with integrity; and 3) God is bringing all the resources and personnel needed together to see the dream become a reality.

In the summer of 2007, I founded a church consulting firm called Sauls Consulting Services (SCS). It was an exciting time, but it was also a very challenging experience. A year before, along with a couple of close colleagues, I had tried to start a church consulting firm. These were incredibly gifted friends and guys that I could see myself working with for the rest of my life. Before we ever went public, I felt a leading from the Holy Spirit that it just wasn't the right time for me to move out of the established firm I was in and move to this start-up. So, before we even got started, I sold my part of the company to one of my friends. Right idea, but the wrong time.

If my relationship with these guys had not been so firmly cemented, the false start could have crushed us. But God used the experience and the misfire to create a desire in me to someday have a "boutique" church consulting firm. It's a story that has a somewhat ugly start but ends with God's will being accomplished in my life, and maybe more importantly, in the lives of my friends. During the next year, God began to mature the dream in me to build a firm that would be based on personal, solutions-based consulting as opposed to program-driven consulting. God was maturing the dream in me as I re-surrendered myself to His will. It was not easy at times, but the pay-off has been a beautiful thing to experience. Second, God was growing me as a consultant and business owner. I had pastored for years and had spent the last seven years of my life consulting with about seventy-five churches across America. Now, God was growing me in a new area in preparation for this adventure. I needed to "get good" in the area of managing a company. I had been so busy on the road doing consulting that I had not taken into consideration the daily operations of running a company. But, in that year between the false start and the beginning of Sauls Consulting Services, I began to spend my time on management and running an organization. Last, in that year, God brought together people and resources for me to start SCS debt-free.

Through a series of meetings and relationships, God brought an incredible Christian rock band into my life. They are heard every day on the radio, but now they wanted to start a missions organization that would reach into Asia, particularly China. I had some of the greatest experiences of my life as I traveled with them and for them to Canada, China, and Tibet. In the six months I worked for them, I saved everything they paid me to get this missions organization up and running. Little did I know at that time that this would be the money that I would use to get SCS going with no debt. God had brought the people and resources together in that year of waiting.

That was the trifecta for me. God made me wait a year to see the dream of SCS come to fruition—not bad in light of Abraham's twenty-five years or Moses' forty years. Re-surrender will take patience, perseverance, and trust that God is at work in your life and in His time will bring His dream to fulfillment in you and through you.

Abraham saw Isaac as the vessel by which God's dream and vision would come to past in his life. God wanted to know if Abraham would continue in his lifestyle of trust. He was being asked to offer up his dream, his child. Over a thousand years after this event, the writer of the book of Hebrews would say, *"By faith Abraham, when he was tested, offered Isaac as a sacrifice. He who had received the promises was about to sacrifice his one and only son, even though God had said to him, 'It is through Isaac that your offspring will be reckoned.*" Then, concluding that God was able to raise him up, even from the dead, if necessary.

Isaac was a literal living sacrifice and Abraham trusted God with what He had entrusted to him. It was in this act that he met the Lord as his provider in the midst of surrender. God desires to be the provider of your life and lifestyle. Can you trust Him with your deepest dreams and loftiest visions?

3. Believe that God will bless, multiply, and give you a great legacy. In Genesis 22:15-18, It says, "Then the angel of the Lord called to Abraham a second time out of heaven and said, *'By Myself I have sworn, says the Lord, because you have done this thing, and have not withheld your son, your only son—blessing I will bless you, and multiplying I will multiply your descendants as the stars of the heaven and as the sand which is on the seashore; and your descendants shall possess the gate of their enemies. In your seed all the nations of the earth shall be blessed, because you have obeyed my voice."*

Early on in Isaac's life, it would have been the custom of Abraham and Sarah to surrender or dedicate their newly born son, Isaac, to the Lord. In this story, we see a life of surrender illustrated. It was not an event of his infancy. Here, we see Isaac once again being surrendered to the will of God. It is this lifestyle of surrender that causes me to use the term "re-surrender."

Because Abraham was able to hold Isaac with an open hand and say, "God, you have entrusted me with my son, but he belongs to You," the results were blessing, multiplication, and the greatest legacy recorded in scripture. That is why many major religions traces its roots back to Father Abraham.

Re-surrender is not an event in your spiritual life; it is a journey toward discovering God's good, pleasing, and perfect will for your life. It is a journey that is marked with mile markers that continually call us back to the place where we once initially surrendered everything to God.

On one occasion, David approached this whole ownership issue by saying this, "But who am I, and who are my people, that we should be able to give as generous as this? Everything comes from you, and we have given you only what comes from your hand," (1 Chronicles 29:14). Now, that is a pretty all-inclusive statement. White flag moments, when we surrender completely to God, are never easy. If surrender to God were easy, everyone would be doing it. However, when we understand that everything belongs to God anyway, it does help to bring perspective to the issue.

Question: If God would ask you "Where are you"—in re-surrendering your dreams, family, wealth, possession, career, education, relationships, marriage, etc.—how would you respond?

Do you hide or do you say, "Here I am."

Do you trust God in the re-surrendering process?

Do you believe Him to be faithful in blessing, multiplying, and leaving a great legacy of faith through your life?

Chapter 3

What Re-Surrender Looks Like

"Sometimes, the heart of desire is transparently clear. Sometimes, it's buried under years of convention, decades of disappointment and lifetimes of fear." - David Gerson

There are times and events in the life of every single person that either opens the heart to surrender or closes it. Surrender is such an act of vulnerability. There is a sense of nakedness. Lord Cornwallis did not even show up for the surrender of his British forces to the American troops at the conclusion of the Revolutionary War.

I do not think it is the sense of shame or failure that marks events of surrender as much as a sense of the unknown and the vulnerability to whomever you are surrendering. The antitheses of all these feelings should mark our complete surrender and continued re-surrender to the One who created us.

God desires close fellowship with you and me. It is what moved Him to search for Adam and Eve in the garden. Fellowship had been broken by sin and disobedience and now God was on the hunt for restored fellowship and re-surrender. It still amazes me that God wants intimacy with me so much that He was willing to sacrifice His son. It further astounds me that He continually seeks me out for fellowship. "Where are you?"

Sometimes, I just want to hide! Yet, true surrender to God and His will for your life happens in his presence. God wants to spend time with you and me. My youngest son, Jonathan, is now away at college. He is about four and a half hours from home and it seems like halfway around the world. Recently, Jonathan came home for Christmas and I found myself wanting to be with him constantly. He is my son!

At nineteen years old, guess what? He had a lot of friends home from college at Christmas and it is amazing how they can stay gone so much on so little money. At least, it seemed he had very little money. He was always asking me for more—not more of my time but more of my money. I get it. But the truth is I still want to be with Jonathan every single moment available. In fact, I find myself very disappointed when he says he is going to do something with me and then all of a sudden, he can't. I know how it works at that age. He plans to do something with me unless something better comes along! He doesn't think I know that but I do.

The point is simply this: I love being with both of my sons. They are my boys. Flawed and imperfect, just like their dad, they are still my boys! Guess what? God wants time with you and me. We are His sons and daughters. Flawed and as imperfect as we are, He still wants time with us.

The act of surrender and re-surrender can only happen in the presence of the One to whom we are surrendering. God wants our attention and he wants intimacy with His sons and daughters. Even more than I want to spend time with David and Jonathan, God "jealously" wants to spend time with you and me.

In Mark 12:30, the scriptures say, *"Love the Lord your God with all your heart and with all your soul and with all your strength."* Loving God so utterly completely means I am "all in," which is a betting term that means, "wagering one's entire stake." Sounds familiar? "All in" means I am willing to surrender everything, in love, to the One who made me in His image. "All in" to the One who caresses me through the years of unfulfilled expectations that have led to disappointments. "All in" to the One who rejoices with me when my heart is transparent, open, and vulnerable to His gentle touch. "All in" to the One who gently holds me in my "valley of the shadow of death." "All in" to the One who loves in spite of my uninformed notions of who He is.

Are you willing to push everything to the middle of the table and say, "God, I'm all in."? That is a picture of what re-surrender looks like in real life. With God, it is not a risk or a gamble. It is quite the opposite. It is exchanging good for the best. It is truly believing and demonstrating that you believe God has the best plan for your life and all that He has given to you to manage.

I know my sons love me; I just want them to spend time with me. I want them to believe that I always have the best intentions for them and their futures. I want them to believe that I think they are the greatest. I want him to believe that I want them to achieve at the highest level and know that I believe they can. Both of my sons are winners. I just want them to intimately know that I truly believe that about them and I want face time with them. Not just phone calls or texts or emails. I want to look at them and feel them with me.

It is really cool when Jonathan calls me and I do not have to initiate the contact. I love it when he pursues me. David, my oldest son, calls me everyday of his life. He pursues me. Guess what? I like it. In fact, he has called me twice while writing this chapter. Do you think it gets on my nerves? No! I have spoken to so many fathers that wish their twenty-four-year old son would call them once a week, much less every day.

We do not always have something "earth shattering" to say to each other. That is not the point. The point is we have fellowship and intimacy because we love each other and we spend time with each other. I would not trade it for anything!

God is not hard to find. Proverbs 8:17 says, "I love those who love me, and those who seek me find me." My sons find me because they seek me, whether it is by phone or showing up at my house. God just wants you to show up. Re-surrender happens as we show up. God is always there.

Re-surrendering Family

Once again—and this is not the last time I will say this: re-surrender is not some event filled with emotions and tears although those things could be a part of it. Re-surrender is an ongoing act of my will to be in intimacy and fellowship with the One who filled my lungs with breath.

Maturing as a Christian father means that I live in the perpetual motions of surrender when it comes to my sons. I can put them on the altar one day, and it seems the very next day I am taking them right back off the altar! The bigger picture here is that God allows me to father my sons and model for them what it looks like to live a continual life of surrender.

Let's look at Father Abraham again on this subject. Genesis 18:19 says, *"For I have chosen him, so that he will direct his children and his household after him to keep the way of the Lord by doing what is right and just, so that the Lord will bring about for Abraham what he has promised him."* Interestingly enough, the Hebrew word for "parent" is the same word that is used for "teacher." As you and I have heard it said so often, "values are caught, not taught." Truth is, it is both. We are always teaching and our children are always "catching," even when we wish they were not.

Abraham was chosen by God to establish His covenant at that time with mankind. He was also chosen to be an example of how God wants to teach and guide His children. The pattern was set from the beginning of God's relationship with His creation. The vital role of parenting and teaching is seen so clearly throughout God's Word.

As the head of your household, it appears from scripture that you must be willing to continually surrender your family to God. Moses said it like this in Deuteronomy 6:6-7, *"These commandments that I give you today are to be upon your hearts. Impress them on your children. Talk about them when you sit at home and when you walk along the road, when you lie down and when you get up."* The lesson learned from the history of God's people in this matter is, as long as Israel's families obeyed the commandment, they prospered. The strict adherence of many Jews to this principle through the centuries has preserved their race long after many others disappeared. Conversely, disobedience to this command has invariably caused chaos and destruction of lives and families.

In Isaiah 39:4, we see a question that is asked of King Hezekiah, *"What did they see in your palace (or house)?"* The answer given by him was, *"They saw everything in my palace.... There is nothing among my treasures that I did not show them."* What does your family see in your home? God's treasures or something else? Are those that live in your home seeing a life of perpetual surrender?

As a parent, I can understand the difficult moments and frustrating times that go with parenting children. Remember that we sow seeds in all areas of our lives, whether it is our children, finances, career, or education. We must understand that we do not reap in the same season that we sow. Paul reminded us in the New Testament that we should not get weary in the process, and if we don't, we will reap a harvest of blessing. So, do not give up!

You can begin a new, surrendered, revolutionary heritage in your family. Pray together. Read God's Word together. Attend church together. Let your family see you in areas of sacrifice and surrender to God. Let them experience sacrifice; let them experience moments of deep surrender. Re-surrender your family to God. This is one great guarantee for building a godly family as you move into a life of full surrender to Christ.

Re-surrendering Relationships

I am a baby boomer who grew up in the height of racial tension in America. Going to high school in the Deep South during the early 70s was no picnic. I was in the tenth grade and was among the first class to go to the "black" high school in my hometown. But, in the midst of all the turmoil that surrounded our daily classes and our nation, I was able to forge some relationships that have even extended to this day. In fact, I recently reconnected with an African-American lady who was in my tenth grade biology class. Will the wonders of Facebook ever cease? God bless Mark Zuckerberg?

The Word of God is a textbook on relationships. At the heart of every page is the message of reconciliation. The life of Jesus exemplified this matter and as Christians, we must be involved in the ministry of building lasting relationships. It always amazes me when I sit in my parent's church in Wilson, NC, and see a congregation that is vibrant and growing. It amazes me because it is about fifty percent Caucasian and fifty percent African-American. This is the same town where, growing up in my early years, I can remember an African-American family being asked to leave the worship service because "We don't have 'colored's' in our church." Now, there is a statement that made an impression upon a ten-year-old kid. I have not forgotten the look on the family's face until this day. In fact, I still cringe as I write about this incident in my young life. If the discussion of this subject makes you feel a little uneasy, then you need to read it very carefully.

Apostle Paul understood this subject as it related to his culture. In Colossians 3:11, he touches on four major areas that had traditionally been separated in his day: race (Greek or Jew), religion (circumcised or uncircumcised), culture (barbarian or Scythian) and economy (slave or free). The answer to every challenge in our society and culture is Jesus Christ living through us! It is a surrendered life of devotion that truly sees the value in every single person God has created.

A life of reconciliation starts in a perpetual heart of surrender. The primary issue should not be race, religion, culture, socio-economic standing. At the cross of Jesus Christ, we all stand equally guilty. That is why the cross stands for all as a means of reconciliation with God and others. Paul wrote in Galatians 6:10, *"Therefore, as we have opportunity, let us do good to all people, especially to those who belong to the family of believers."*

Likewise, the ministry of reconciliation must extend to those who are outside the family of God. The cross of Jesus Christ is not a protected property of the church, any one nation, any particular race, or any economic segment of society. It belongs to every single person and we are called to a surrendered life that shares this life-giving message to anyone and everyone.

Do you want to live a surrendered, revolutionary life in Christ? Begin by re-surrendering your relationships to Him today. Build bridges and overlook differences. Live your life as if you are the only Bible some people will ever read. You may well be, you know?

Surrender Does Not Mean Defeat

Is it really possible to live a life without sin? That is a question that brings out the worse in so many doctrinal and theological camps. Here is what I do know: living a life without sin seems incredibly attractive, but yet so unattainable in our human frailties and desires. Apostle Paul, in 1 Corinthians 15, talks about how our bodies of "weakness" have yet to be raised in "power." The sinful nature of humankind is a powerful magnet that often wins the war of the spirit and flesh.

Yes, we have the promise that one day our corruption will put on incorruption, and sin will finally be fully defeated in our lives. But, in the meantime, we are told, *"If we claim to be without sin, we deceive ourselves and the truth is not in us. If we confess our sins, he is faithful and just and will forgive us our sins and purify us from all unrighteousness,"* (1 John 1:8,9). It is my experienced observation that re-surrendering daily (often) is the key to a life of victory. You see, surrender does not have to signal defeat. In fact, quite the opposite is true. It is impossible to live a victorious life without surrendering and re-surrendering often. In the case of the Christian life, the "white flag" signals victory, not defeat. It signals strength, not weakness.

The power to live victoriously is available to us moment-by-moment, day-by-day, because of what Christ accomplished on the cross. In fact, the writer of Hebrews says, *"For we do not have a high priest who is unable to sympathize with our weaknesses, but we have one who has been tempted in every way, just as we are—yet was without sin,"* (Hebrews 4:15). That is the reason we must go to Him continually, for *"He is able to save completely from all unrighteousness,"* (1 John 1:9). Re-surrender every area of your life to him, confess your sins, and ask for forgiveness, strength, and victory. This kind of re-surrendering leads you to be free to enjoy the unfettered fellowship of the Holy Spirit in your life every single day.

John Piper, a wonderful Bible teacher, once wrote, "All things were created by him and through him and for him—even your worst supernatural enemies. In the end, it was they—not Christ—who were shamed at the cross (Colossians 2:15). In the end, everything and everyone serves to magnify the glory of our Savior and increase the gladness of his people in Him."

God desires for us to live victoriously, no matter what challenges we face in life. 1 Corinthians 15:57 says, *"But thanks be to God! He gives us the victory through our Lord, Jesus Christ."* This find of victory is obtained not by humiliation or embarrassment, but by boldly coming to God and confessing, "I need you" and re-surrendering every single facet of your life to Him.

Re-surrendering Our Way To Victory

In 1974, I began a journey that was incredibly exciting and at the same time, disappointing. I will start with the disappointment side first. I began attending Atlantic Christian College, now Barton College, as a music education major. I loved music and wanted to be a musician, not necessarily a music teacher. A musician. More precisely, I wanted to be the next John Lennon. To this day, he is still my favorite Beatle. There was something rebellious and raw about Lennon that truly attracted me to his music, even after he left The Beatles.

Well, I didn't become the next John Lennon; I didn't even become a rock star, which was the ultimate goal anyway. In 1974, just about any kid who had long hair and could rock a guitar wanted to be a rock star.

But God had another idea for my life. I later transferred to East Coast Bible College where I received a B.S. degree in Church Music. Two years later, I went on to get a Masters Degree in Music Education at Winthrop University. During my time at ECBC, God called me to full-time vocational ministry. I must say that initially, I was not very happy and I went kicking and screaming. After all, I still wanted to be a rock star. I know this will shock my mom and dad, but the truth will set us all free. Sorry you had to read it in this book!

This was the first occasion in my life that I truly had a big moment of re-surrender. It was no small thing to set aside my secret ambitions to be a rock star, and say, "yes" to a life of ministry. I do not think anyone who has served in ministry for any reasonable amount of time would say that it is a lifestyle of glamour only eclipsed by the life of a rock star. Now, I'm not looking for sympathy. I am just stating the facts as it looked to a twenty-year-old at the time. The truth is, the gift of music that God had given to me had to be stewarded in a way that pleased the Owner of the gift, Jesus Christ. It was given to me to manage, not to own. Music could not ultimately land in my "ownership" category; it belongs to God. I am the manager, but He is the owner.

Victory at that moment back in 1978, has translated into many incredible moments of ministry throughout the last thirty-some years. By the way, from this end of life, I would not go back and trade God's calling on my life for the life of any rock star. I am doing what God shaped and created me to do. It does not get any better than that!

One of the things I learned in Music Theory 101 is that A-440 or Concert A is the 440 Hz tone that serves as the standard for musical pitch. The term literally means that the A above Middle C = 440 vibrations per second. For example, a violinist tunes his or her instrument to A-440 to make sure he or she is in tune. Once the A string is tuned, all the other strings can be adjusted to play harmoniously together. Otherwise, the result would be a cacophony of chaos, which you can find naturally in atonal music, such as the works of Arnold Schoenberg. His twelve-tone technique leaves something to be desired in the world of harmony. But, that's a whole other subject for another time of discussion.

Violinists know they must tune their strings often, knowing that an accidental bump or simply playing the instrument can result in enough variation to cause discord, or out of tune playing. Likewise, it is easy to get out of tune, or out of sorts, as humans. Christ is the A-440 or the standard. If we are not in a right relationship with Him, we can expect other relationships to be out of tune. We either vibrate in harmony with Him, or we slide into dissonance. Pick up a guitar that has not been touched for quite some time and strum the notes. Not a very pretty sound is it. Sometimes our lives, as reflected in our relationships, can sound like an old, out of tune guitar.

1 John 3:23-24 says, *"And this is his command to believe in the name of His Son, Jesus Christ, and to love one another as he commanded us. Those who obey his commands live in him, and he*

in them. And this is how we know that he lives in us: We know it by the Spirit he gave us." How do we stay in tune with God? It starts with living a re-surrendered life in Him and walking in obedience to what He has called us to do and made us to be. We must allow Him to tune us to His perfect pitch. The Bible is very clear on this: *"And whatsoever we ask, we receive of him, because we keep his commandments, and do those things that are pleasing in his sight* (1 John 3:22).

As a follower of Jesus Christ, it is important that we stay tuned to His life in us. It starts by first confessing that He truly is the "perfect pitch" and for our lives to be lived in harmony with Him and others, we must stay tuned to Him consistently. Once again, re-surrender is not an event; it is a lifestyle or spiritual journey that is to be enjoyed along the way. *"Let us fix our eyes on Jesus, the author and perfecter of our faith, who for the joy set before him endured the cross, scorning its shame, and sat down at the right hand of the throne of God* (Hebrews 12:2).

Section 2

How Do I Know It's Really God?

"The Christian should have an appetite for prayer. He should want to pray. One does not have to force food upon a healthy child. Exercise, good circulation, health and labor demand food for sustenance. So it is with those who are spiritually healthy. They have an appetite for the Word of God, and for prayer."

- Dr. Billy Graham

Chapter 4

Hearing God's Voice

In this spiritual journey that God has called us to live, I have suggested that the first mile marker is taking all my plans, dreams, hopes, gifts, talents, abilities, etc. and daily laying them on the altar of God. Re-surrender is a step in the right direction. However, it is not an event in our lives filled with emotions and chill bumps. It is an on-going act of surrender that continually leads us toward a deeper fellowship and relationship with the Creator of the universe.

Oh, and by the way, I think re-surrender to God is a difficult first step, but one that is worthy of our deepest devotion. There is another mile marker that grows out of re-surrender and becomes our second mile marker, and that is hearing God's voice.

Our culture is constantly flooding us with messages from the various media outlets. Communication has never been easier and more instantaneous. It used to be dominated by movies, books, television, newspapers, billboards, commercials, and advertisements. Now, you can add smart phones, iPads, laptops, Twitter, Facebook, blogs, and the list will grow by tomorrow.

There has never been a time when our attention has been so fought for by the media and marketing firms of our nation. I am not even complaining; I enjoy most everything that is in the list above. But, with so many "voices" coming at us these days, how do we even begin to distinguish the voice of God when He is trying to get our attention.

There is a clear case to be built that God wants to speak to us and He wants us "to get it." John 10:27 says, *"My sheep listen to my voice, I know them, and they follow me."* On one occasion while in Israel, and specifically Bethlehem, the tour group I was with came up on a couple of shepherds and they had sheep and goats in their herds. There are two things I noticed that day as we observed these shepherds with their flocks. First, the sheep knew the voice of their particular shepherd. It was amazing to watch as one shepherd would call his sheep and some of the flock peeled off and followed his voice. Then when the other shepherd spoke, the remaining sheep followed him. These sheep knew the voice of their shepherd and when he spoke, they listened and followed him in obedience. Second, while the sheep obediently followed their shepherd, the goats just continued to wander in ignorance. As sheep of His pasture, we are called to hear his voice and follow in obedience. But, to follow the voice of the Shepherd, we must be able to distinguish His voice.

God obviously wants to speak to us and desires that we listen to what He has to say. And, as for me, if the God who created the universe and breathe life into my body has something to say to me, I think it is pretty important that I listen. There are a few things I truly want to get right in life, and I know this is one of those things.

Back to my story in the Philippines, one afternoon as I was relaxing in my room, I decided it was a good time for me to get in some prayer time and spend some uninterrupted moments with God. After some time of prayer, I truly sensed that God was speaking to me about my ministry. Specifically, He was speaking to me about a change in my ministry. This caused quite some consternation in my spirit because I had been at my church at this time for over thirteen years. I felt very comfortable in ministry, loved the people of our church, loved our small community, and felt like I could finish out my ministry there.

In addition to that, my boys loved their lives. After all, they were PK's. That is pastor's kids for those of you who may not know this exotic ministry terminology. They were born there and were very involved in the local sports community. We were only a couple of hours from my parents' home and since their retirement, they had become great baby sitters for us.

It has always been a challenge for me to clearly distinguish God's voice in my life. I'm a talker and I love to communicate. But I'm not necessarily a very good listener. It is pretty difficult for me to slow my mind down and truly listen to what it is that God is trying to communicate to me. My mind is always spinning. I'm always thinking, and although I know the importance of two-way communication with God, I'm not that good at it.

On this day, though, I was trying to distinguish the words of God as He was speaking to me about the direction of my ministry. Now, understand I'm a "self-talker." I talk to myself quite a bit. Not out loud, but nevertheless, there is some significant communication going on, even when no one is around. So do you, just admit it. The task was truly not to say something to myself that I wanted to hear, but to listen with a quiet spirit to what God was saying to me. As I have thought back on this moment over the years, God was saying that He wanted to change my ministry from pastoring a church to pastoring many churches and pastors.

The context of this moment was so fitting. Here I was in the Philippines working with pastors and churches in the area of church growth. God was using this moment to set me up for a major change in my ministry and life.

I did not understand what God was suggesting, but since I had listened to Him early on when He called me to public ministry, I knew His voice and I was willing to listen. I knew this was going to call for radical changes so I decided to let it simmer in my spirit over time and see if God would open doors for me. Quite honestly, not only did He open doors, He eventually had to kick me through the doors. It seemed obvious to people closest to me, but I guess I was too close to the situation emotionally to "get it."

Well, by the end of that year, I had resigned my church, moved to Atlanta to work with a church consulting firm, and on the road working with pastors and churches across America. It was what God had spoken to me during my time in the Philippines and it fit my personality and gifts very well, but I still needed some help during that year of waiting to get me moving in a positive direction. It took positive and negative circumstances in my life to get me going.

That year between hearing God's voice and God moving in my life became a "testing time" for me. Would I truly listen to what God was saying? Would I be able to distinguish His voice? Would I allow God's timing to work in my circumstances? Would I allow emotions and comfort to dull the voice of God in my life?

With thousands of voices coming at us each day and demanding our attention, it is important for us to understand those voices and, ultimately, to discern God's true voice. First, the most obvious voice that wants to direct our lives is our own. That is what I earlier referred to as "self-talk." My mind is a powerful voice in my life. The mind tells us what to think, our will tells us what we want, and our emotions tell us what to feel. Apostle Paul says it like this, *"Those who live according to the sinful nature have their minds set on what that nature desires. But those who live in accordance with the Spirit have their minds set on what the Spirit desires"* (Romans 8:5). In the words of that great theologian (just kidding) and country music singer, Zac Brown, "Our mind tells our heart what our mouth should say." The mind is so powerful and that is why it is so important to have a "renewed mind" as Paul talks about in Romans 12:2. Our minds and emotions are so unreliable. Self-talk is so unreliable. It is critical that we learn to distinguish the still, small voice of God as He speaks directly to our spirits.

Second, the voices of people all around us are trying to continually get our hearts and minds. As a pastor, it was amazing how many people had a "word from the Lord" for me. Now, I'm not discounting that and I do believe that God uses people to confirm things in our lives that He is saying to us. But I also believe that God can speak to me directly and if I'm willing to listen, I will be able to discern what He wants to communicate to me. As those people spoke to me about their "word from the Lord," it was uncanny how often their messages to me had nothing to do with what God was saying to me at that time, but looked very familiar as part of their agenda for my life.

God does speak through other people into our lives, but there are many "other" voices that are destructive and not well meaning. So, how do you know it is God? Years ago, I was working with a church in Massillon, OH. My youngest son, Jonathan, had heard me speak about the church and was very aware of what was happening at Grace Community Church. So, one day I'm getting ready to leave for Ohio and he sticks an envelope in my hand. Inside of it was a note and $100 in cash. His note went something like this: "Dad, I want you to give this to Pastor Michael and don't try to talk me out of it. God told me to do this. Jonathan." I knew Jonathan had saved the money for quite some time. It was money from his allowance, some birthday money given to him, and some money he just found lying around the house that was unclaimed. I knew there were things Jonathan wanted and yet he wanted to give it to this church because he had heard God speak to him. What a great lesson of hearing God's voice and not letting other voices, including his dad, talk him out of what God wanted for his treasure.

Maybe his reward for listening to God's voice and not allowing anyone to talk him out of it came about six months later. I was consulting with a church in Green Bay, WI and one of the families in the church discovered that my birthday was in October. They had been waiting for twenty years for the family Packer tickets to be passed down to them. This was their year! They gave me two tickets positioned eleven rows back to see the Green Bay Packers play the Baltimore Ravens, at the time the defending Super Bowl champs. Jonathan was a huge fan of Brett Favre so I took him with me for the weekend.

We went to the game and it was just an incredible experience. All in one afternoon, we got baked by the sun, it hailed on us, it rained on us, and at the end of the day, we nearly froze to death. Yet, we had the time of our lives as we watched the Packers defeat the Ravens. My son had the opportunity to see his favorite player lead his team to an incredible victory. If that is not enough, that evening the church I was consulting with had an event at Brett Favre's Steakhouse, which was about two blocks from Lanbeau Field. Upon arriving at our event, we found out that the whole Packer team was celebrating their victory together in the next meeting room. We walked by and saw Favre sitting in the back with his traditional red worn-out hat.

Later during the evening, I was speaking and noticed my son was not in the room. When I finished, I asked someone if he knew where Jonathan had disappeared to during my very interesting talk. Someone said he saw him go to the men's restroom. Later, I found out from Jonathan that he had excused himself and went to the restroom where he bumped into Brett Favre. He had about a ten-minute conversation with him, but Jonathan later told me, "I didn't shake his hand, Dad, because we were in the bathroom." I cannot prove it with empirical evidence but I choose to believe that God rewarded my son for listening to His voice, not being talked out of what he heard, and living it out in obedience.

Third, there is a voice that you will hear early, often, and long. That is the voice of the Accuser. The devil is a very crafty communicator. On one occasion according to the Bible, he was able to deceive one-third of the angels of heaven into rebelling against the greatness of God. It was the devil in the Garden of Eden who spoke to Adam and Eve and his deception has brought about unspeakable pain and consternation in our fallen world.

Most often, Satan appears to us in our thought life and he tends to distract us with a barrage of ungodly messages in order to bring confusion into our lives. The Bible teaches us that he seeks to overwhelm, terrorize, seduce, and do whatever it takes to destroy you and your loved ones through his messages. It is no wonder God tells us, *"Be self-controlled and alert. Your enemy the devil prowls around like a roaring lion looking for someone to devour"* (1 Peter 5:8).

Fourth, thankfully God wants to speak and is speaking to you and me daily. Distinguishing the voice of God comes from spending time with Him. It is easier to separate out the unfamiliar when you personally know the familiar. So, how familiar is the voice of God in your life? Have you learned to distinguish the sound of His calling?

Most of us want to hear God through supernatural, spectacular, sensational, and scintillating words. God seldom speaks that way. He seeks to direct our lives through His presence, His Word, prayer, His Spirit, and even, sometimes, through the circumstances of our lives.

Let me show you how God uses circumstances on occasion in our lives. I had a pastor friend who had been trying to connect me with a very high profile pastor in Atlanta for about a year. He knew that pastor needed the services that my company offered and he felt I could truly help his friend's church. I tried for a year to get us connected but his pastor friend is very busy pastoring a huge church with three campuses. One Sunday he sent me a text that this pastor was committed to talking to me the next day and that I should give him a call on his cell phone. Quite honestly, I had very low expectations of getting in touch with this very busy pastor. Anyway, the next day I was on a flight to Dallas and really did not have time to connect with this pastor. On Monday, as I sat in my middle seat on this flight, I was working with my iPad and paying very little attention to those around me. I felt a man come and sit next to me on the plane, but I did not even look up from my work. After some time, I glanced over and saw the man was reading a book on preaching. I asked him if he pastored a church. He said yes and told me the church he pastored. Then he introduced himself to me by name. He was the pastor that I had been trying to get connected to for a year. And there he was, seated next to me. I had almost two hours to tell him about SCS and how we could partner with his church. After some time, he just looked at me and said, "I need you to help me." God had truly moved through my circumstances to make happen what would have never happened if I tried to force it.

Guidelines That Open Us To Hearing God's Voice

In one of his many books on prayer, Dr. David Cho writes, "Prayer is a dialogue, not a monologue. To pray effectively, we must listen to God as well as speak. Since God has called us into a loving relationship, we must see the importance of what that kind of relationship entails. Whether hearing God's Word in a better understanding of the scripture or His divine direction for our lives, knowing how to listen to God is extremely important."

Listening to God's voice is so critical to the intimacy and fellowship that God wants to have with His creation. His voice brings clarity to the roadmap that He has placed in front of us in this spiritual journey. Here are a few thoughts or guidelines to help you better listen for God's calling.

First, to hear God's voice, you must have the right mindset and attitude. In John 7:17, Jesus speaks to us about what that attitude looks like: *"If anyone chooses to do God's will, he will find out whether my teaching comes from God or whether I speak on my own."* Jesus shows us the importance of a right attitude. It is a choice we make. God speaks to people who have already determined to do what he says. God will speak to you in your dilemma, if you have already determined that what He says you will do.

If you have already determined in your mind and spirit that you're not going to act on what God says to you, whether it is overt or not, you probably will never truly hear the clear, small voice of the Holy Spirit speaking to you. Your attitude is critical to hearing the voice of God.

The second principle is similar, and it is to "have an ear to hear" the voice of God. Most people who have any relationship with God hear His voice from time to time, but they don't really hear Him. Jesus was speaking to His disciples on one occasion and He said, *"'Listen carefully to what I am about to tell you: The Son of Man is going to be betrayed into the hands of men.' But they did not understand what this meant,"* (Luke 9:44-45). They heard Him speak, but they did not really hear Him. Why did Jesus have to tell these guys to listen *carefully*? This was God standing there in the flesh. Wow! You would think every time He opened His mouth it would be an E.F. Hutton moment.

The reason His followers did not hear what was clearly being said by Jesus was they didn't have an "ear to hear." They had physical ears to hear, but not spiritual ears to hear. They heard but their closed spirits kept them from truly hearing what He was communicating to them. As long as Jesus performed miracles and manifested the power of His future kingdom, they were willing to understand and listen, at least to the temporal implications of what Jesus taught. But when they were told they would lose their Messiah and Lord, they shut down.

More than one person has told me on more than one occasion that I have selective hearing. I tend to hear what I want to hear and totally miss something that might mess up my day. The disciples were not interested in listening to the possibility that Jesus would be taken from them, so they practiced selective hearing.

Has God ever spoken to you about something in your life? Maybe it was a person or a habit that the Spirit of God was warning you to beware. It was not outright rebellion, but you just chose to practice selective hearing. "Well, if I act like I didn't hear His voice, then I don't have to be responsible or accountable for what He said."

Having an "ear to hear" is to have the capacity to understand what God is saying with a proper attitude that says, "I must act on what God is saying to me about that situation." That proper attitude is simply obedience and we will talk more about that subject in the next section.

There is a third principle that will help us in hearing the voice of God and it is to purpose in our minds to listen attentively when we are in prayer. We must find a way to still our racing minds, soften our hearts, and quiet our spirits so we can hear the still, subtle voice of God. It is just really hard to pray effectively when you are on the run.

One of the best ways to put this into practice is to purpose that during your prayer time you will have a time of stillness and solitude. It seems to be a practice that we see in the life of Jesus, *"Very early in the morning, while it was still dark, Jesus got up, left the house and went off to a solitary place where he prayed,"* (Mark 1:35). In the Bible, there are other examples of people who did a similar thing. We see it all through the Book of Psalms with David. Isaiah talked about listening to God in His temple (Isaiah 6). In Acts 10, we see a picture of Peter as he slipped away to the roof of a house and God spoke to him in a dream. The Scripture is full of other accounts of people who took time in their private devotions to just listen carefully. If it was important to Jesus that He should hear the voice of the Father and it took a private, quite place, then it might be important that we follow His example.

How Can I Know Those Leadings I Am Hearing Are From God?

One of the most asked questions I heard as a pastor was, "How do I know the voice I'm hearing is God's and not Satan's or just self-talk?" I think there are some guidelines that we can look at for testing leadings and voices we are often hearing during our times of solitude and prayer. First, are the leadings you are hearing consistent with God's Word? God's unrevealed will for your life (those areas that are a little nebulous) will always line up with His revealed will for your life that is found in the Bible. God will never tell you to do something that is contrary to what His Word says.

On one occasion, while pastoring, I had a lady from our congregation make an appointment to see me concerning something that was going on in her marriage. After explaining to me the situation for quite some time, she really got to what she wanted to tell me. "Pastor, God is telling me to leave my husband." I am not suggesting there aren't some extreme situations that might cause one to have to leave a marriage, but her situation did not qualify. In fact, she was just listening to the wrong voice or voices in her life.

Second, I believe the leadings we get from God will typically be consistent with the person He has made you to be. As I heard one guy say, "What God has called you to do, He has equipped you to do." God is purposeful in every action He takes. Now, He does love to stretch us out of our comfort zones, but He does not ignore the gifts, talents, abilities, personality, and inherent interests He has placed inside of you. That is what uniquely makes you, you. He has poured all these unique areas of giftedness into your life so you can serve Him more effectively and efficiently. It does not make sense that God would contradict himself in this particular matter.

If you are sensing a leading in your life that seems so completely contrary to who God has made you to be, you need to test it very carefully. It could be that God is stretching you and testing you in an area that He wants you to demonstrate faith and obedience.

However, it could be Satan or self-talk that is getting you off the spiritual journey that God has uniquely designed for you.

One more thing: These leadings that the Holy Spirit drops in our hearts typically require an element of servanthood. So, if a leading or a voice you are hearing is promising you overnight health, wealth, comfort, or happiness, you should be very cautious about moving forward.

God led His son, Jesus, to a cross, not a crown. And yet, that cross ultimately proved to be the gateway to freedom and forgiveness for you and me. Test it first; then walk after it in obedience to God.

Chapter 5

A Journey To Wisdom and God's Presence

"Lay hold of my words with all your heart; keep my commands and you will live. Get wisdom, get understanding, do not forget my words or swerve from them. Do not forsake wisdom, and she will protect you; love her, and she will watch over you. Wisdom is supreme; therefore get wisdom. Though it cost all you have, get understanding."

Proverbs 4:4-7

God's leadership in my life through the years has been the major indispensable element that has kept me moving forward in faith. Occasionally, I enjoy taking control and after a few "scrape ups" and "wrecks," I humbly ask God to fully take back the helm of my life. I have been blessed to have great educational opportunities over the years and feel I have good common sense, and those are gifts and opportunities from God. However, when I am left to direct my life, I find that I am constantly in "deep weeds." I know I need God's leadership in my life.

God's wisdom is the ultimate roadmap to follow in moving toward fulfilling all that God has for our lives. A road or path is a common example throughout the Bible. Wisdom points us in a way that moves us toward living a God-honoring life. Conversely, I tend to stumble rather often when left to my own wisdom and direction.

So, if wisdom is that important and truly marks the road that God has for my life, how do I obtain and put into practice this wisdom that comes from the Lord? We need to understand that true wisdom is not a result of the number of years I have lived, but it is a result of time spent with God. One of the wisest men who ever lived wrote in Proverbs 2:6, *"For the Lord gives wisdom, and from His mouth come knowledge and understanding."* One of the wisest pastors I have ever met is about fifteen years younger than me and every time I get around him, I learn something new. Godly wisdom is not related to age, but rather a desire to be with God, hear His voice, and act on what he is saying. It is not some educational process or some book we read. As Solomon says, "the Lord gives wisdom…."

If it is true that God gives us wisdom, then I think we should be asking Him for it. James 1:5 says, *"I any of you lacks wisdom, he should ask God, who gives generously to all without finding fault, and it will be given to him."* Here's a thought: Why don't we just ask God to give us wisdom? I think if we value godly direction on this journey we are on in life, we will ask Him and desire wisdom with all of our hearts. In other words, having wisdom must be a value in our lives.

When was the last time someone asked you the values you live by, and you immediately say, "Well, the number one value in my life is pursuing and thirsting for godly wisdom." Once again, in writing about wisdom, Solomon says in Proverbs 2:3-5, *"If you call out for insight and cry aloud for understanding, and if you look for it as for silver and search for it as for hidden treasure, then you will understand the fear of the Lord and find the knowledge of God."* Solomon says that you should put on the "full press" to seek out the wisdom of God, which begins with the fear of the Lord. It should mark our lives as a value for which we stand.

Psalm 19:7 tells us, *"The law of the Lord is perfect, reviving the soul. The statutes of the Lord are trustworthy, making wise the simple."* The greatest wisdom we will have obtained in this life is found by reading the Word of God.

Godly wisdom comes from understanding the source of wisdom, asking for it, valuing it in your life, and studying and applying the Word of God.

Entering God's Presence

> *"O God, you are my God, earnestly I seek you; my soul thirsts for you, my body longs for you, in a dry and weary land where there is no water. I have seen you in the sanctuary and beheld your power and your glory. Because your love is better than life, my lips will glorify you.*
>
> - Psalm 68: 1-3

In this passage, David paints such a vivid picture of his desire for intimacy with the Creator. He understood that the initial move toward true intimacy with God is moving from the flesh to the soul. In the Old Testament tabernacle, the flesh is likened to the sacrifice for sins in the outer court. Every studious Hebrew understood this fact. Inside the sacred tent, curtained away from the outer court, was the inner court, or the Holy Place. This is the place of the soul or inner desire. The Holy Place was twenty cubits long and ten cubits wide. It contained the table of shewbread, the golden candlestick and the altar of incense—each with specific significance.

Inside the Holy Place, ten cubits square, was the Holy of Holies, which contained the Ark of the Covenant, a sacred chest that was a symbol of God's divine presence. A veil of very costly material divided the Holy of Holies from the Holy Place. No one except the high priest was allowed to enter the Holy of Holies and he was only permitted to enter once a year, on the Day of Atonement.

However, at the death of Christ on the cross, everything changed for you and me. Matthew 27:50-51 says, *"And when Jesus had cried out again in a loud voice, he gave up his spirit. At that moment the curtain of the temple was torn in two from top to bottom. The earth shook and the rocks split.*" Christ's death signaled the opening of a new and living way to the presence of Almighty God. Before, the veil kept people from coming into the most holy place where the presence of God rested.

The price of intimacy with God was paid in full, yet so few Christians are willing to do what is required to enter into the Holy of Holies. It begins, as David indicated in Psalm 68, with a thirst and hunger for an intimate relationship with Christ. Apostle Paul said, *"Let us therefore come boldly to the throne of grace, that we may obtain mercy and find grace to help in time of need."* To sustain this journey, it will depend on a desire from us to be intimately involved with God. It is accessible to anyone on the journey who is willing to listen to God's voice and desire intimacy with Him.

Carol, who is very close to me in life, had a radical salvation experience when she was in her late 20's. Sitting in her townhome in New York City, drinking at the time, the Holy Spirit came to her and convicted her and she fell to her knees and asked for God's forgiveness. Today, she has an incredible love for God and for His wisdom in her life. She pursues his presence daily with all her heart. And I will say about her, she is wise way beyond her years. She is an incredible woman who truly loves God with all her heart. She is educated, brilliant, but more than those things, she is discerning and intuitive, and truly hears God's voice regularly in her daily life.

Chapter 6

Hearing Is Believing

If it is true that the Creator of the universe wants to have a relationship with us, His prize creation, then how does that happen? What does it look like? Many people, including Christians, believe that God is silent and that He has muted Himself toward His creation. They are saying that, yes, God created us, but now He has left us to our own paths, journeys, troubles, disappointments, victories, etc. It doesn't sound like a very compassionate Heavenly Father, does it? In fact, it does not sound like a God that I want to serve with all my heart, soul, mind, and strength.

The Bible is clear that if we will truly seek God and hunger for a relationship with Him, we will enjoy the fruit of that search. Proverbs 25:2 says, *"It is the glory of God to conceal a matter; to search out a matter is the glory of kings."* It appears that the glory of God is concealed through His Word, but anyone can see His glory revealed through careful searching of His Word. The Bible is replete with earnest seekers who traveled the path of discovery and found God.

The Word of God is like a treasure to be discovered and truly enjoyed. I'm reminded of the scene in *National Treasure* when Nicolas Cage discovers the hidden treasure deep in the hills below Mount Rushmore. It seems the deeper the treasure, the more valuable it is. The deep truths cannot always be mined by merely scratching on the surface of God's Word. It is as though God the Father has given us mile markers on this journey that points us toward the ultimate treasure, His Son, Jesus Christ.

To obtain this kind of intimacy and worthy treasure, you must be willing to dig beneath the surface and explore the paths that may seem difficult at the moment. But, at the end, there lies a treasure worthy of exploration and sweat. That is why it is so important to ask the Father to give supernatural wisdom as you search the scriptures for fresh, priceless, life-giving resources on a regular basis.

The Psalmist describes the Word of God as a lamp unto our feet and a light unto our paths. He also writes in Psalm 18:28-31, *"You, O Lord, keep my lamp burning; my God turns my darkness into light. With your help I can advance against a troop; with my God I can scale a wall. As for God, his way is perfect; the word of the Lord is flawless. He is a shield for all who take refuge in him. For who is God besides the Lord? And who is the Rock except our God."* The Word of God is flawless. It is perfect to guide you and me on this journey toward what God has called us to be and made us to be.

It is the Discovery Guide for discerning God's good, pleasing, and perfect will for our lives. While there are several ways to hear the voice of God, all certainly valid means of gaining godly guidance, there are none that is as reliable as the scriptures. Every other means of hearing from God must be measured by what God's Word has to say.

The Bible is God's revealed will for our lives. Most everything that you will ever need to know about God's will for your life is in His Word. However, I understand the argument that it is just not specific. Really? How specific do we really need it to be? I believe God has revealed more of His will for our lives than we will ever get accomplished.

So, how much do you need? I do believe God speaks to us in other ways and gives us His unrevealed will for our lives. But it starts with the scriptures. What does God's Word say about you and your destiny?

God's Word can truly illuminate our lives. It will direct our paths as we move through this journey of life. It is full of mile markers that we will need to hit. We should purpose to spend time with God through reading and studying His Word. It is the most reliable guide on this journey to God's will and purpose for our lives. It is capable of taking us from a place of uncertainty to a victorious life in Jesus Christ. The Bible will enable us to conform to the image of our Savior as we seek to hear Him speak into our daily lives.

Prayer: Two-Way Communication

Most of us know what it is like to spend time in prayer and listen for the voice of God, and then spend considerable time deciding, "Now, was that God or was that me?" Discernment is a critical element in hearing God's voice as He speaks to you on occasions.

The ability to discern the voice of God is tied so closely to our intimacy with God. When one of my sons call me, I don't need to hear more than "Hey, Dad," to know who it is. And, it's not because one of them calls me dad that I can identify the caller. Immediately, I know both of my sons' voices. Although they sound very similar, I can immediately identify whether it is David or Jonathan.

That happens because I am intimately involved in their lives. I know their voices and they know mine. We immediately connect because we have spent hours and years together. Even further, they know my voice so well that in just a few moments, they can tell if the conversation is going to go well or not. We have all had those kinds of conversations with our parents. As well, when they call me, I can tell if this is going to be a conversation about money or some other subject. Maybe it is just a dad thing. The point is I know their voice; they do not have to identify who is on the other end of the conversation.

The story is told that during the First World War, a British soldier was caught one night while creeping secretively back to his tent from a nearby wooded area. He was immediately hauled before his commanding officer and charged with holding communications with the enemy. The man pleaded that he had gone into the woods to pray. That was his only defense.

"Have you been in the habit of spending hours in private prayer?" his officer asked roughly.

"Yes, Sir," said the soldier.

"Then you get down on your knees and pray now like you've never prayed before!" the commander ordered.

The young man knew he could be shot at sunrise for the crime he was accused of committing. He knelt and poured out his soul in a powerful prayer that could have only been inspired by the Holy Spirit.

"You may go," the officer said in hushed tones after the soldier finished praying. "I believe your story. If you hadn't drilled often, you couldn't have done so well at review."

The young man had a breakthrough that saved his life. He did so because he had prepared for that breakthrough for some time, not knowing what challenges he would face. He had learned to commune with God intimately.

When we pray, there are some things that happen in our lives that otherwise just will never come to pass. Prayer has the ability to reveal who we really are in light of who God is. The revelation of self is always followed by a revelation of God and His mercy.

Prayer also brings cleansing to our spirits. As you confess your sins and failure to God, He cleanses you from your unrighteousness and failures, allowing you to come boldly into His presence with a pure heart. And prayer reveals the Word of God, allowing Him to lead, direct, and illuminate our journey. Psalm 119:18 tells us, *"Open my eyes that I may see wonderful things in your law."*

As that commander said about the young soldier, it will be so fulfilling if we would "drill" often, in preparation for the times when we will truly need to seek God and hear His voice.

When we pray and read God's Word, we become so familiar with who God is, and the more we understand who He is, the easier it is to distinguish His call on our lives.

Listening To The Spirit

There was an incredible promise made by Jesus in the first chapter of the book of Acts. This promise basically says that in the absence of Jesus in the flesh, He would send the Holy Spirit who would literally take up residence in our lives. In other words, Jesus promised that He would send the Spirit of God and He would live inside of us to lead, direct, and guide our journey.

If you truly want to understand how this works in your life, then I encourage you to read and reread a passage of scripture that is found in Romans 8:11-16. *"And if the Spirit of him who raised Jesus from the dead is living in you, he who raised Christ from the dead will also give life to your mortal bodies through His Spirit, who lives in you. Therefore, brothers, we have an obligation—but it is not to the sinful nature, to live according to it. For if you live according to the sinful nature, you will die; but if by the Spirit you put to death the misdeeds of the body, you will live, because you did not receive a spirit that makes you a slave again to fear, but you received the Spirit of sonship. And by him we cry, 'Abba, Father.' The Spirit himself testifies with our spirit that we are God's children."* Read it again and again until you gain a confidence that comes from knowing that because you are a son or daughter of God, you have His Spirit living in you. What confidence it gives me when I understand that God, the Holy Spirit, lives inside of me and He is there to direct my journey.

So, how do we hear the Spirit of God living inside of us? Can we truly distinguish it from self-talk? In 2 Corinthians 13:14, Apostle Paul writes, *"May the grace of he Lord Jesus Christ, and the love of God, and the fellowship of the Holy Spirit be with you all."* Now, what does that mean?

I think we have to understand again that intimacy and fellowship comes from spending time in the presence of God. Whether it is reading His Word, praying, listening, they all require that we spend time with Him and as we spend intimate time in His presence, we begin to understand His heart for us. We begin to understand His intentions for our lives. We begin to understand that He has a plan for our lives and as the scriptures tell us, it's a plan to make us prosper, not to harm us. God has chosen to pour out His love *"into our hearts by the Holy Spirit, whom he has given us,"* (Romans 5:5).

Fellowship with the Spirit also implies participation with Him as we invite Him into the plans of our lives. The Holy Spirit wants to become our partner in all the events and activities of our lives. Fellowship also includes friendship where the Spirit of God wraps His intimate arms around us in love, and through that expression, we sense His presence even in the midst of storms in our lives.

There is also a sense of camaraderie that comes from fellowshipping with the Holy Spirit. One of the Greek meanings for "fellowship" is the word "commander." The Holy Spirit wants to be our captain, a loving and caring commander who provides instruction and direction for the journey. And fellowship and intimacy with the Holy Spirit gives us power to share what God has uniquely done in our lives. In fact, Jesus simply said it like this in Acts 1:8, *"But you will receive power when the Holy Spirit comes on you; and you will be my witnesses in Jerusalem, and in all Judea and Samaria, and to the ends of the earth."*

So, are you spending intimate time listening for the voice of the Holy Spirit? If He spoke to you, have you spent enough time with Him to distinguish His voice from self-talk. Recognizing His voice requires spending time with Him and hearing him speak to you often.

Can God Use Circumstances To Speak?

I heard a quote some years ago by Sir William Temple that says: "When I pray, coincidences happen; when I don't they don't." I am often amazed as I look back on my life how God used circumstances and coincidences to get me to the place He wanted me to be. I can just see His DNA all over the history of my life. I did not even like some of those circumstances at the time, but now it is amazing how hindsight is 20/20.

After graduating from a small college in North Carolina, I truly wanted to go on and work on a master's degree. It was a small Bible college and not many graduate schools were lining up to take students from this institution. But, there was one in Rock Hill, South Carolina that would accept me. The problem was I was serving a church in Burlington, North Carolina, which is a long way from Rock Hill, South Carolina.

One evening at home in Burlington, I received a call from the church in Rock Hill, SC, asking me if I was interested in serving there. Within two months, I was serving this church, which was five blocks from the university, and enrolled in the graduate school. I could not have made that happen! I know I am not that good. But, through some incredible circumstances at the church in Rock Hill, God opened a door for me to serve there for eight years. In 1981, two and a half years after moving there, I received an M.M.E. from Winthrop University. The degree allowed me to also teach at the small undergraduate college that I had graduated from in 1978. Wow, talk about circumstances.

In the book of Matthew in the Bible, there is the story of the birth of Jesus and the unusual circumstances that unrolled that persuaded a group of men to come and be a part of the Christmas story. Now get this, *"After Jesus was born in Bethlehem in Judea, during the time of King Herod, Magi from the east came to Jerusalem and asked, 'Where is the one who has been born King of the Jews? We saw his star in the east and have come to worship him.' ...and the star they had seen in the east went ahead of them until it stopped over the place where the child was. When they saw the star, they were overjoyed,"* (Matthew 2:1-2, 9-10). What an unusual set of circumstances God designed to lead the wise men to the birth of Christ!

The nearest planet to earth is thirty-seven million miles away and the nearest star is twenty-five billion miles away. Whatever light the wise men saw, traveling at 186,000 miles per second, had actually exploded at least five years prior to the birth of Christ for the sight of the explosion to reach earth. Some would call this star a mere circumstance. Just as God gave the wise men an illuminated path to follow on their journey to Jesus, in His perfect plan, we can trust the path He has mapped out for us on this journey.

Can God use circumstances in our lives? Absolutely! Are they the most reliable way of hearing God's voice and gaining His direction? Probably not. That is why it is so important that we test circumstances and coincidences to see their validity in the light of who God is and the plan He has for our lives.

Proverbs 3:5-6 tells us, *"Trust in the Lord with all your heart and lean not on your own understanding. In all your ways acknowledge him, and he will make your paths straight."* This promise assures us that if we truly trust Him and understand that listening to ourselves is highly unreliable, He will take responsibility for our lives and direct and guide us along the journey.

We can learn, through intimacy with God, to recognize His hand and voice through both positive and negative circumstances; however, circumstances are not always an indicator of God' plan for our lives. Maturation comes as we become less vulnerable to circumstances in our journey, for we know the promise found in Psalm 37:23-24 that say, *"If the Lord delights in a man's way, he makes his steps firm; though he stumble, he will not fall, for the Lord upholds him with his hand."* Whatever circumstances happen, we can know that God is in control of those circumstances.

Section 3

The Fight Toward Obedience

"[The natural life] knows that if the spiritual life gets hold of it, all its self-centeredness and self-will are going to be killed and it is ready to fight tooth and nail to avoid that."

- C. S. Lewis

Chapter 7

So...You Want Me To Do What?

"God's commands are designed to guide you to life's very best. You will not obey Him, if you do not believe Him and trust Him. You cannot believe Him if you do not love Him. You cannot love Him unless you know Him.

- Henry Blackaby

I was sitting in a Chick-fil-A restaurant in John Creek, GA about five years ago when God spoke to me in the way that He typically speaks to me. It was just a simple leading dropped in my heart by the Holy Spirit. It was nothing earth scattering and the request God was making of me was not going to change the world.

He simply said to me, "Give that lady twenty dollars." That is it. I am sorry if you thought it was going to be some life-changing, mind exploding command of me. That is all it was. Now, I knew whom He was talking about because I had been observing this little Hispanic lady who was cleaning the dining room of the restaurant. She looked so pleasant and seemed to be at peace with who she was. In fact, I was thinking I wished I felt what she seemed to be feeling.

At that time, I was facing some big decisions in my life and I truly did want to hear what God had to say about it. However, on this occasion, He was seemingly unconcerned about me and the situation that was causing some sleeplessness in my life. At least, that was the true feeling I had as He spoke to me. So, I reasoned with God as I sat there and said to Him, "No problem. I do not mind giving twenty dollars to this lady. I am sure she can use it." At this time in my life, twenty dollars just did not seem like a very big deal and I love to give. No issue!

But, I did ask God if it would be all right with Him if I first finished my Chick-fil-A sandwich on wheat, no pickle. I didn't hear anything so I just assumed no news is good news. I would finish my sandwich and then I would find her and give her the money. After all, I am a pretty quick eater and it would not take long for me to take care of this sandwich.

Probably fifteen to twenty minutes later, I was finished and looking for the little lady to give her the twenty dollars and impress God with my benevolence. I looked around the restaurant and did not see her. I knew the manager/operator of the restaurant, so I went to him and asked him, "Gene, where's the little lady who's always cleaning around here?" motioning to him that she was very short. "She timed out about ten minutes and she has left to go home," Gene said.

It's a simple story, but it illustrates a fact that is so true in my life and maybe in yours. It is one thing to hear the voice of God as we talked about in the last chapter. It is another to be obedient to His voice. For me, in this case, delayed obedience became disobedience.

There is a huge chasm that often exists between hearing God's voice and executing His commands or leadings that He drops in our spirits. As much as I want to hear God's voice, He wants me to act in obedience with what I hear.

The motivation for obedience flows out of a heart that has been overwhelmed by the incredible love that God has for us and our reciprocated love to Him. It has to begin with believing that God's intentions toward us are to bless us and provide us with life to the fullest on this planet and in the hereafter. You cannot believe Him for that kind of life unless you love and trust Him. And, as I have talked about earlier in the book, that kind of love and trust comes from building a relationship with God that flows out of intimacy and allows you to distinguish His voice clearly. That is truly what makes the journey worth traveling.

There is incredible joy in this journey when you enjoy taking the ride with the One that loves you the most. I have never enjoyed getting in a car and driving long distance by myself. But I don't mind the drive if there is someone with me whose company I truly enjoy.

Fred Franks is a dear friend of mine. He is vice president of Sauls Consulting Services, Inc. I first met Fred when he was pastoring in the San Francisco area. He had hired me to work with him on a major construction project that his church had undertaken. Have you ever been around someone just a little while, and you are thinking to yourself, "We click!" Well, that is what happened. That was in 2005 and since then, Fred and I have become best friends. Outside of my sons and family, there is no one in the world I would rather be around.

I truly have a couple of other guys I feel that way about—Dr. Paul Lanier and Ed Carroll—but I don't live very close to either of them. Fred now lives across the street from me in Atlanta. One night he was walking across the street back to his house from mine, and he just turned around and looked at me. We were thinking the same thing. It is incredible that we live across the street from each other. We are best friends, in business together, and golf partners. It sounds like a commercial, but it truly is "priceless."

Fred and I have a church we are partnered with in the Nashville, Tennessee area. We have traveled to Nashville several times together. It is about a four-hour drive. I don't like driving and I don't like riding very much, but the time goes by so fast in the car when we travel together. We talk, sing, and laugh. Fred is one of the few guys who can sing the old 70s rock and roll stuff and still sing southern gospel with me. Sometimes, one of us will just start singing an old gospel song and the other just jumps right in and never misses a beat. Well, he can't sing harmony, but I enjoy taking the tenor part.

That kind of intimacy is possible in the life journey with Jesus. There is incredible joy in this sometimes-tough journey, when you truly experience God's presence with you.

Obedience becomes so much easier when you realize that God truly "is for you," and not against you. Believing that God wants the best for you and He can truly bring joy to your journey makes listening to His voice and obeying His voice so much easier and fulfilling.

What Keeps Us From Obedience?

What is it in our lives that keep us from obedience? Self-centeredness and comfort quite often keep us from obeying God in ways that would truly please Him. However, I do believe there is one more thing that keeps many of us from being a "Just Say the Word" follower of Jesus, and that is FEAR. The fear factor has kept many good men and women from just doing what Jesus says.

The fear of failure consistently limits people from fully reaching their potential in Christ. It's this kind of fear that leads us to say things like, "What if I really did obey God, and then I messed up?" Or, "What if I decided to truly follow Him, and He asked me to give up something I dearly love?" Or, "What if I decided to be completely obedient to God and my family just laughed at me?" The questions go on and on, and you've either asked them at times or you know someone who has done it.

Kay Arthur has this to say about the fear of failure: "So many times, we can't serve God because we aren't whatever is needed. We're not talented enough or smart enough or whatever. But if you are in covenant with Jesus Christ, He is responsible for covering your weaknesses, for being your strength. He will give you His abilities for your disabilities."

Many people know what it is like to have fear grip them and rip the fabric of their relationship with Jesus. The inside voice often sounds like this: "Don't even bother trying this thing because you can't do it. Besides, what if you try and fail? Your friends and family will laugh at you."

The fear of failure is often associated with the "paralysis of analysis." We can over think something that we are hearing God say to us. So, we get bogged down with, "Now, was that the voice of God or is that self-talk? Am I just saying to myself something I want to hear?" Over thinking a leading can take us down the path of "delayed obedience," which is a form of disobedience. Most often, a delay on acting on a leading from God is disobedience in our lives. And, it may lead to a window of opportunity that quickly closes and we just simply miss it.

When David and Jonathan were younger, occasionally I would ask them to pitch in around the house. That means I would assign them a chore and ask them to get it done. Sometimes, there would be a window of opportunity to get that chore completed. If it didn't happen during that time of opportunity, I would consider them as being disobedient to me.

Not only does the fear of failure keep us from being obedient to God, but also, believe it or not, the fear of success has kept many people from simply obeying God. "What if I obey God and supernatural things just start happening in my life? What will people say? What will my friends think? Are people going to think I am some kind of Jesus freak or weird?"

It is so easy, after we have had some measure of success in being obedient to God, to begin to believe "our own press." Somehow, we think we did it or we can do it on our own. Success can breed a sense of self-reliance that causes us to move away from obeying the

One who gave us gifts, talents, and abilities to accomplish what He's called us to do.

There is also a fear of other people that truly has caused many Christians to shrink back from great "God challenges and opportunities" in their lives. There is a fear that many, if not most, of us will face at some point in our lives and that is, "What will my friends think of me? What if this caused me to lose that promotion at work? What if this caused my buddies to kick me out of the foursome?" If you value someone's opinion of your life and the way you live it, then you know what I am thinking about in this case. Particularly, people who tend to be "people pleasers" struggle when it comes to other's opinions of your spiritual depth, or lack of it.

The real question then becomes: Do we live for an audience of One or for the audience of those that surround us in life? In most cases, it doesn't come down to an either/or decision. But, if it does, can you make the right "obedience" decision?

Have you ever been concerned about what the future holds for your life? Have you ever taken to the extreme, where concern became fear? Pastor Steve Robinson says it like this: "When God asks us to do something that doesn't make sense to us, we can begin to think of all of the future implications associated with obeying God."

Imagine the fear that Abraham must have faced when challenged by God to sacrifice Isaac on the altar, "But God, if I obey you, my son Isaac will die. And you couldn't fix that problem." Still, Abraham overcame the fear of the future without Isaac by trusting the goodness and provision of God. In fact, according to the writer of Hebrews, he believed that God would raise his son from the dead if needed.

And then there is a story in the Old Testament of a guy named Joshua, who was facing what looked to be insurmountable challenges in what God had called him to do. Joshua had served as the protégé to Moses for many years, but now Moses was dead. God has given leadership of His people over to a young Joshua to lead them into the Promised Land.

Joshua had to make a choice: Would he obey the voice of God or play it safe? Moses had already "dropped the ball" on this one and he was a seasoned leader. At some point, he must have thought to himself, *Wow, Moses couldn't pull this off, how will I ever do this?* Joshua came to the conclusion that with God, it could happen and God's ability could make up for the lack of his experience.

Faith Over Fear

What do we do to overcome the fear of failure, success, other people, and the future and advance on in the journey? First, always believe that God is for you. God is our perfect Heavenly Father and the scriptures remind us that He wants to give good things to us. Why? Because we are His sons and daughters. He loves us, and He is for us. He sees our failures and He reminds us that with our Father, "all things are possible." He knows all our successes and He reminds us that we did not do it in our own strength. He feels when we are frightened by relationships and reminds us "He is a friend that sticks closer than a brother." He is omniscient and He already knows our future, and He has promised to "make our paths straight." Jesus is close and He is for you.

I have loved this verse in Jeremiah since I was a young teenager trying my best to follow Christ even though I had the typical fears of a youth, *"'For I know the plans I have for you,' declares the Lord, 'plans to prosper you and not to harm you, plans to give you hope and a future,'"* (Jeremiah 29:11). The omniscient, omnipotent, omnipresent God of this universe has a unique plan for your life and it includes a future that He has designed for you. John Henry Newman says, "God has created me to do some definite service; He has committed some work to me which He has not committed to another. I have my mission—I never may know it in this life, but I shall be told it in the next."

Along the journey, quite often, the signals get switched when pertaining to faith and fear. It could be a challenging situation with a parent, a coach, or some other authority figure in our lives. Rather than the message of Jeremiah 29:11, we get a message, "You will never amount to anything" or "You're worthless" or "Can't you do anything right?"

Not only do we begin to question the validity of our lives, we begin to question the goodness of God. Is God good? Does He love me? Does He even know me? Does He truly care about me? Satan wants us to do that. He wants us to question the very nature and character of God. It is his plan to create doubt concerning our value to God and the uniqueness of which He has created us.

R. A. Torrey writes, "It is true that He does sometimes require of us things that to others seem hard. But when the will is once surrendered, the revolutionized life plans become just the plans that are most pleasant, and the things that to others seem hard, are just the things that are easiest and most delightful. Do not let Satan deceive you into being afraid of God's plans for your life."

Let me remind you one more time: God is for you. He loves you and has a unique plan for your existence. He wants to be the Provider for you, and He is always mindful of who you are and where you are.

The second decisive step that you must take in overcoming all types of fear is to shut out the opposition, whether it is Satan or other people. When you decide to do something significant for God, Satan will tell you that you cannot do it and others will remind you of your past. Quite often, those seemingly closest to you really do not want you to do something Herculean for God. That only reminds them of how safe they are playing it with their faith.

Remember the story of Joshua and his mission to take the children of Israel into the Promised Land? Ten of the twelve leaders that he had sent on a secret mission into the Promised Land came back and said, "Hey, the inhabitants in the land are big, and we can't overtake them." In essence, Joshua's response to his leaders was, "God is bigger than the giants or any obstacle. I think we will move forward."

Quite often, we must start with just shutting out the opposition—whether it is from Satan, family, friends, or whoever it is that you are allowing to speak into your life. Now, that does not mean we don't listen to wise counsel. This gets down to others' agendas for your life. You have to ask yourself: Can they be truly objective in this area? Do they have a hidden agenda for me? Do they truly want God's will to be accomplished in my life? Do they love me? Do they truly care about obedience?

It is important that you do not presume on God and think that if everything is positive, it must be God. Conversely, do not think that because there is opposition, it isn't God. Charles Swindoll says: "When you suffer and lose, that does not mean you are being disobedient to God. In fact, it might mean you're right in the center of His will. The path of obedience is often marked by times of suffering and loss."

Apostle Paul was beaten and left for dead, snake bitten, caught up in hurricane-like storms, thrown out of cities, wrestled with his weaknesses, struggled with complicated relationships; the list of "suffering and loss" goes on and on. Yet, he was in the center of God's will for His life to take the life changing message of Christ to the Gentile world. What if he had questioned God's will because of suffering, or even inconvenience?

We have to believe God is for us, shut out formidable opposition that is not honoring to God and His call on your life, and third, be proactive and do what it is that God has called us to do. You must hear the voice of God, confirm it in the scriptures, in prayer and through godly counsel, and then, step out in faith, trust, and obedience.

Imagine the consequences for the human race if Abraham did not step out in faith concerning the sacrifice of his son, Isaac. Imagine the plight of a couple of nations if Joseph had not listened to God and saved grain for the impending drought. Imagine the world if Jesus had not been obedient to die on the cross. Our eternities would never look the same.

Surround yourself with your own "personal advisory board." Be very careful and selective on who you will allow to be in your inner circle because they will have tremendous influence in your life.

The people you choose for your group will be the people you will be listening to for wisdom and advice. Get a picture in your mind of three to five people you would like to sit on your "personal advisory board." Can you see them? Those people you are going to be listening to are a preview of the "future you."

Here are three questions that you should be asking yourself as you determine action steps on what you believe you are hearing from God. First, are the action steps you are taking consistent with the scriptures? Remember, the scriptures contain God's revealed will for your life so action steps of obedience cannot violate what God's Word says. Second, is this decision consistent with the godly counsel you are receiving from your "personal advisory board?" As you are choosing your "personal advisory board," you will want to choose those that are exemplary of where you want to be in your future. And last, are these action steps of obedience consistent with how God has uniquely shaped you? God has uniquely made you to accomplish certain things in life. It truly is your life mission. And, what God has called you to do, He has uniquely equipped you to do with certain gifts, talents, abilities, experiences, and passion.

We all look for the "happily ever after" ending. We all want the miracle, but it appears that obedience always precedes the miraculous in the affairs of human beings. It is a common thread that we see weaved throughout the Word of God. God told Moses, take off your sandals in the book of Exodus. Because he was obedient and did something as simple as removing his shoes, God empowered him to lead the children of Israel out of four hundred years of slavery. All because he showed humility and obedience in the desert with something as simple as removing his shoes in the presence of God.

God told Noah in Genesis 6 to build an ark for the salvation of his family. He just did it, in spite of the humiliation he faced from friends and others who just laughed at him. But, because he was obedient, God did the miraculous.

God told the leper, Naaman, in 2 Kings 5, to go and dip seven times in the Jordan River. Because of his obedience, God did the miraculous. He was a leper. His skin was falling off his skeleton, but because he chose to obey, God supernaturally healed his body. Jesus told Peter to walk on the water to him and Peter obeyed him and he walked on water. He was obedient and God did the miraculous.

Obedience is never easy. If it were, everyone would be doing it. Obedience takes commitment and you do not drift into commitment. You have to purposely commit to what God has called you to do and made you to be. Once you have committed, obedience is not nearly as difficult. But it does truly take trust and understanding God's plan for your life.

Chapter 8

Understanding And Participating In God's Plan

"The word of the Lord came to me, saying, 'Before I formed you in the womb I knew you, before you were born I set you apart; I appointed you as a prophet to the nations,"
(Jeremiah 1:5).

These are the word of the Lord as he called Jeremiah as a prophet to speak to "*nations and kingdoms.*" In this chapter, it literally says that God reached down and put His words in Jeremiah's mouth. He says to him, "Do not be afraid of anyone, because I am with you. I'll tell you what to say and you do not need to be fearful."

Jeremiah carried out God's plan for His life, but it doesn't mean he never questioned or felt overmatched. And, neither will you. As we walk in obedience to God's plan, he truly wants us to understand it. God is all about revealing His plan as you are able to handle it.

God is intricately involved with the smallest decisions and cares of your life. Matthew 6:32-33 says, *"So do not worry, saying, 'What shall we eat?' or 'What shall we drink?' or 'What shall we wear?' For the pagans run after all these things, and your heavenly Father knows that you need them. But seek first his kingdom and his righteousness, and all these things will be given to you as well."* Now, I didn't put that passage in here because you've never seen it or heard it. You probably skipped over it and went on to the un-italicized words. But remember, obedience is grown out of trust, and you can only trust someone if you believe they have your best interest at heart. So, go back and read the passage one more time. God cares about the small, intricate portions of your existence.

God also cares about the choices you are facing right now in life. They may not turn out the way you want them to, but it does not mean the choices escaped God's care and plan for your life. *"For this God is our God for ever and ever; he will be our guide even to the end,"* (Psalm 48:14). In my self-talk and self-pity, there are times that I want to think God is not paying attention and just doesn't care. The psalmist reminds us that He will direct us "even to the end." There are even times that my mind tries to convince my heart that God is not really in control. Maybe, somehow, He lost His sovereignty and needs my help. Once again, the psalmist says that He is "God for ever and ever."

You may not need to know that personally right now. Things may be going perfectly in your life, personally, professionally, and financially. But, trust me, you will need to review Psalm 48:14 at some time. Mark it now! Maybe not today, but maybe tomorrow or next week or next month. You will need the assurance that God is God and He wants to be in charge of your life.

God truly cares about the decisions we make and He wants those decisions to reflect His will and direction for our lives. Ephesians 5:17 reminds us, *"Therefore do not be foolish, but understand what the Lord's will is."* God is not trying to secretly hide His will from you. He wants you to know it more than you do. Don't make it so hard. Remember these three things: First, God's will is available only through a relationship with Jesus. Our culture tells us that we can receive guidance from a smorgasbord of beliefs and rituals. In fact, the more of these you embrace, the more balanced your life will be. Jesus was a lot more exclusive and said, *"I am the way and the truth and the life. No one comes to the Father except through me* (John 14:6). If you don't stand for something, you'll fall for anything. Make a decision that you will grow your relationship with God systemically and watch how He reveals His will to you.

Second, you must offer your life up as a "living sacrifice" to God to truly know "His good, pleasing and perfect will." His design and plan for your life is revealed as you settle the great stewardship question of your life. "If God owns it all, what am I doing with it?" Management of God's gifts, talents, and abilities reflects the understanding of God's will for your life. So, how are you in the area of spiritual management?

Third, your mind must be reshaped by God's touch if you are going to discern His will for your life. Romans 12:2 says it like this: *"Do not conform any longer to the pattern of this world, but be transformed by the renewing of your mind. Then you will be able to test and approve what God's will is—His good, pleasing, and perfect will."* So, how does that happen? It comes by spending time with Him and in essence, laying our lives on the altar. That is the "open hand" aspect of our lives. We are continually re-surrendering everything to God.

There is an old hymn that dates me well back. The writer says, "Trust and obey, there's no other way, to be happy in Jesus, but to trust and obey." Trust will lead to obedience. And, obedience allows us to discern God's plan and then execute it as He empowers us. As we walk continually in obedience, it makes the journey of life more enjoyable and fruitful.

Understanding God's will is one thing, and it is truly important. Participating is quite another thing and it often leads to some incredible adventures. The writer of Hebrews says, *"May the God of peace, who through the blood of the eternal covenant brought back from the dead our Lord Jesus, that great Shepherd of the sheep, equip you with everything good for doing his will, and may he work in us what is pleasing to him, through Jesus Christ, to whom be glory for ever and ever. Amen* (Hebrews 13:20-21). I still do not get it completely, but I do know that God's Word tells us that He has uniquely equipped His children with gifts, talents, abilities, personalities, etc. and then, He works in us to see His will accomplished in and through our lives.

I was having a conversation with a close friend this week and the statement I made to him truly reflects my whole life. I have never been great at anything, but I have been blessed to be good at a lot of things. I have often wondered what it would be like to be a Tom Brady or Peyton Manning and be the very best at your profession. I watched Aaron Rodgers in Super Bowl XLV and thought, *He's got the world at his feet now*. He is at the top of his craft.

God uniquely gifts all of us in the body of Christ; some are great at what they do while others are good at a lot of things. But, we all have gifts, talents, and abilities that we will be hold accountable for on the Day of Reckoning. We see this so clearly in Matthew 25 with The Parable of the Talents. In this case, talents are a measure of finances in that day.

The owner has called in three of his employees and has given them a measure of money to manage in his absence. It says, *"He entrusted his property to them."* That is exactly what God has done with us, as He has invested in our lives. He has entrusted us, in some case, with a family, wealth, career, health, spiritual gifts, etc. and we have the privilege of managing these things.

As this story goes on, we are told that this owner has given each of them talents, but of varying amounts. To one, he has given five talents, to another two, and the last one, he gave him one talent. Because he is the owner, he can give each one whatever he wants and there should be no argument from those that are managers of his possessions.

The "sin of comparison" has hurt many well meaning Christians and in turn, has hurt churches in which they serve. "If I could speak like Jim, I would be out there doing God's work all the time." I don't think so. If you are not using what God has given to you, you probably will not steward other gifts very well either. "Well, if I could sing like Sara, I would sing all the time for God's glory." What are you doing with what God has entrusted to you? What are you doing, right now, with what God has given to you to grow you and bring Him glory.

Some people are "five talent" people in the body of Christ. I'm not, but I do know some who are and they manage it very well. Some are "two talent" people and I probably fall into this category. After pastoring for twenty-two years in local churches, I feel very confident and just as anointed now as a church consultant. I feel I am making a difference and I have the privilege every year of working with five and six great churches across America and assist them in seeing their God-given dreams come true.

As a consultant, I do two things well. I have been blessed to mentor and teach in the area of leadership and stewardship. I believe these are two key ingredients in the growth of the Kingdom of God. Leadership will sustain the future of your ministry, while stewardship will fuel it. You need both and I have truly found my niche in God's kingdom.

By the way, there are "one talent" people in the body of Christ. Here are the two things that all three people had, and still have, in common: The talents did not belong to them; they were only asked to manage the talents. Second, they had to give account for how well they did in the management process.

Here's one more thing for you to think about: Five-talent guy or gal did not have to give an account for two or one-talent guy or gal. Two-talent guy or gal did not have to give an account for one-talent guy or five-talent guy. You get it! We are held responsible to give a good answer to God on the Day of Reckoning for only what He has given to us.

So, Jesus is standing there eye-to-eye, toe-to-toe with you and there's no one there to plead your case this time. There's no Johnny Cochrane. The One that died for you and gave you the talents you have says to you, "What did you do with what I gave you?" Wow! I want to have a good answer for that one. If I've ever been ready for an exam, that's the one I want to ace. God doesn't seem to grade on the curve. I want to participate fully in what God has for me in this life.

Archimedes, upon discovering the power of the lever, said, "If you find me a fulcrum to rest my lever upon, I can move the world." God desires to reach the world, and He has chosen to use you and me to do it. However, to participate fully in His plan requires faith in the plan and an active belief that sustains us in carrying out that plan.

Too often, there is a huge chasm between our belief and our behavior. We say that God wants to work through our lives, but we fail to get involved with the plan He has for us. One of the Greek meanings of New Testament words "faith" and "belief" is fulcrum. With faith, we have a lever. With that fulcrum, we can be a participant in God's divine plan for this world.

We must understand there is a difference between faith and believing. That difference means everything as we seek to participate in God's plan for our lives. Believing is faith in motion. It means applying the truth that I know in my heart about God. Faith helps me to put confidence in God and exercise what I know to be true.

Faith is God's gift, but believing requires my will. It is a gift just the same as breathing, walking, hearing, and seeing. However, just as God does not breathe, walk, hear, or see for me, neither does He believe for me. He has given me the capacity to believe in Him, and requires me to actively participate in whatever He directs me to do.

Faith and believing become stronger as I exercise them in my life. Conversely, they also tend to become weaker when I neglect to use them. As I participate in God's plan for my life, I find my faith growing and belief expanding for my divine mission in life.

Faith and believing are limitless. You cannot exhaust God's ability to work in and through you. The smaller your dream is for your life, the less you need God to show up. But, if you have a dream so big that if God doesn't show up, you're in the tank, then you are beginning to step out into faith territory. That is where God wants you and works best through you. It is impossible to say you did it if it is a huge deal. No one will believe you anyway. But, if it is so big that God had to work through you, your friends will be saying things like, "Wow, God had to do that! That is so big. He could have never done that. I know him. He's not that good. God had to show up in his life!" Now, that's faith territory. That is where God wants me to be. That's truly participating in God's plan for your life.

One last thought on productivity in God's Kingdom. You can involve yourself in too many things and get outside of your "productive zone." You should focus on the things in God's Kingdom that has uniquely called you to do and say "no" to things that will not bring advancement for your growth and His glory. When Steve Jobs came back to Apple in 1997, the company had 350 products. Within, one year he had eliminated 340 products and Apple then had ten offerings. By doing this, Jobs said we can put our A-Team on all ten offerings and be more productive as a company. The rest is history!

Find the things you do best and bring your A efforts to those things. As I have mentioned a couple of time in this chapter, it will bring you growth and Him glory.

Chapter 9

It's Not Either/Or, It's Both/And: Rest And Persistence

"He alone is my rock and my salvation; he is my fortress, I will not be shaken," (Psalm 62:6).

Smith Wigglesworth, known as "the apostle of faith," once wrote, "Nothing in the world glorifies God as much as simple rest of faith in what God's Words says. 'This is the work of God, that you believe.' Jesus said, *'My Father has been working until now, and I have been working'* (John 5:17). He saw the way the Father did the works; it was on the groundwork of knowledge, faith based upon knowledge. When I know Him, there are so many promises I can lay hold of, and then there is no struggle, *'for (he) who asks receives, and he who seeks finds, and to him who knocks it will be opened,'* (Matthew 7:8)."

Problems will come and go. Circumstances will change in life. There is a time in the Christian life that you must become convinced that God is in control, whether things make sense or not. With that, comes a conviction that God is sovereign and He can be trusted with all the circumstances of my life. Paul wrote in 2 Timothy 1:12, *"I am not ashamed, because I know whom I have believed, and am convinced that he is able to guard what I have entrusted to him for that day."* There will be times in your life when obedience requires you to do nothing more than to rest in God, fully convinced that God is God.

There will be times when no one can encourage you as you can encourage yourself, reaching deep inside for God's secret, unshakable provision, and assurance. There are not many days that I don't call my mother and ask her to pray about things that are going on in my personal life and business. Sometimes, people can talk to you, counsel with you, pray for you, but, eventually, it comes down to your direct, unfathomable, intimate, solid relationship with the Creator. Thank God for my mom, my dad, and others who have prayed and continue to pray for me daily. But, sometimes, I just have to rest in Christ and realize that it is in Him alone that I can put my faith and trust.

Too often, people have a horizontal worldview of God that suggests limitations and a withdrawnness that would characterize Him as disinterested and distant. Truthfully, God is not lacking in knowledge of all the details of our lives. Resting in Him suggests that we are at peace with who He has made us to be and living in the circumstances He has allowed to surround us at any given time.

We live in very difficult and stressful times, stoked by the price of fuel and groceries, uncontrollable crime, a fluctuating market, a fully distressed housing market, not to mention what goes on daily in the Middle East. When we look at the worst of things, especially all the issues of our culture, we can find ourselves agitated and pressured. God wants us to rest in Him in spite of the circumstances that surround us. Somehow, we must become compartmentalized. We should not deny the difficulties around us like the plight of the hurting and homeless. At the same time, we must learn to lean into His presence in our daily lives and rest in Him.

God has given us a better way, a clear revelation of how we can rest in His presence by truly building our lives of the Rock of all ages. Paul said it like this: *"Consequently, you are no longer foreigners and aliens, but fellow citizens with God's people and members of God's household, built on the foundation of the apostles and prophets, with Christ Jesus himself as the chief cornerstone,"* (Ephesians 2:19-20).

I was reminded of this so vividly not long ago while vacationing in the islands. I was standing on a rock that was elevated some five to six feet above the water. The waves were crashing against it consistently and pretty hard. I could actually see the sand shifting as the tide waves rolled in and back out. I felt completely secure as I stood above the waves and shifting sand on a rock that absolutely seemed unmovable.

Christ is our unmovable Rock; we can place our faith in Him until we know that He is completely worthy of our unshakable faith. At that point, you can truly rest on the Rock, although crazy things may be going on all around you. Your friends and family may look at you and question how you are surviving, and you can point to the rest that you have found in an unmovable Rock that sustains your soul.

Priceless Lessons Of Persistence

We live in an "instant" culture. I have found myself annoyed using my iPad because I had to resort to 3G, instead of the WiFi connection. I know it must have taken me at least twenty seconds longer to download a file. We have little tolerance for anything that requires our time, patience, or persistence. We should not be surprised that too often, we have the attitude that our relationship with God should be something like a cosmic vending machine— "Do it, God, NOW!"

There's a passage in Luke 18 where Jesus helps us understand that there is a place in our Christian walk for sheer persistence. *"Then Jesus told his disciples a parable to show them that they should always pray and not give up. He said, 'In a certain town there was a judge who neither feared God nor cared about men.*

And there was a widow in that town who kept coming to him with the plea, "Grant me justice against my adversary.' 'For some time he refused. But finally he said to himself, 'Even though I don't fear God or care about men, yet because this widow keeps bothering me, I will see that she gets justice, so that she won't eventually wear me out with her coming!'" (Vs. 1-5).

We tend to get so impatient and impetuous because we do not see instant results and we forget God's timing and divine providence are always perfect. We neglect to remember that His infinite wisdom should not be challenged by our human, finite reasoning and expectations. A major element of obeying God is not giving up, even when our faith is not instantly rewarded.

In the story recorded in Luke 18, Jesus illustrated the power of persistence and never losing heart in the battle. He tells this story of a widow who would persistently bombard this wicked judge with her request. Her request was simply for justice to be done. The judge, either too busy or disinterested in her case, would simply say, "Go away!" What was the woman's response? She firmly declared, "No, I am not leaving until you do what I am asking of you." Finally, because of her tenacity, the judge agreed to hear her case because she would not cave in to impatience and living in the moment.

In the next few verses after this, it says, "And the Lord said, 'Listen to what the unjust judge says. And will not God bring about justice for his chosen ones, who cry out to him day and night? Will he keep putting them off?" (Vs. 6-7). Jesus never criticized the woman in the parable for her unrelenting pursuit of an answer from this wicked judge. He did not suggest to the crowd that she lacked faith. In fact, he commended her for our actions.

Have you ever felt like you were annoying God by your persistent requests of Him? This story suggests that we should never give up. Persistence is not at odds with your faith in God and His ability to work on your behalf. Conversely, keep your requests constantly before the Lord. Let Him know you are in this thing for keeps. Don't confuse “not now,” with “no.” Don’t give up. Don’t stop asking. Don’t stop knocking at your Father’s door, for your persistence and patience are powerful steps toward obedience in your life.

Chapter Ten

Obedience, No Matter What!

Some years ago now, I read a book that talked about the revealed and unrevealed will of God for a person's life. It made great sense to me because I like to simplify things down to their lowest common denominator. I want to understand God's will for my life and this simple statement helped me understand that God's will is not a difficult thing to discover.

I was always convinced that it was some mystical thing out there in the cosmos and if I would be good enough and do enough good things, God might let me peek at His plan for my life. I have since learned and am quite convinced that God's will is always around me and He wants me to know it more than I do.

If we are going to be obedient, "just say the word" followers of Christ, it is critical that we have knowledge of what it is that He has in store for us. Obedience begins by becoming completely submissive to the revealed will of God for our lives. That simply means that most of God's will for my life is revealed in His Word and it is my responsibility to read and study the roadmap that is provided for me.

I get to travel quite a bit for Sauls Consulting Services, Inc. Currently, SCS has about seventy church-clents across America from the east to the west coast. Needless to say, living in Atlanta, I have a very close relationship with Delta Airlines. When I arrive in a new city, I typically have already mapped out my way from the airport to the church. I really do not know how we made it before MapQuest, Google, and GPS. Living in a city the size of Atlanta makes your car's GPS your very best travel friend. Can you believe there are hundreds of streets in our city that contain the word "Peachtree" somewhere in the title? Yet, I have never seen a peach tree in the ATL.

God has provided the ultimate GPS for the journey that we are on in this life and it's called The Bible. Psalm 19:7 says, *"The law of the Lord is perfect, reviving the soul. The statutes of the Lord are trustworthy, making wise the simple."* The writer is letting us know that the accuracy of God's roadmap is uncanny. It is perfect. It is trustworthy. I have been in some cities where my little googled roadmap was less than accurate.

Here's the catch for us: There is knowledge and then there is applied knowledge. The more we devote ourselves to God's Word, the more the journey opens up to us and we see God's preferred future for our lives in amazing color. It provides uncanny wisdom and direction to the journey as we engulf ourselves in its unmatched wisdom. The more we study the Roadmap, the wiser we become, and the more we realize that God requires our obedience to His divine instruction found in His revealed will for our lives—the Bible.

Anytime there is a definitive book written on a discipline or subject, it is referred to as the bible of that area of thinking. Why? Because it is the definitive word on that subject. Everything in that discipline is measured by that particular volume of work. It is the bible. It is the definitive word on that subject.

The Bible is the definitive word that eclipses all other volumes written. It is the measuring rod of everything that matters in this life. It is the home of God's revealed will for your life. You will never capture God's will for your life if you do not love, read, and study His Word. It is the definitive collection of wisdom for our roadmap of life.

The Hebrew meaning of wisdom includes separating yourself to God, opening your life to Him, and allowing Him to reveal His roadmap to you. Throughout the Roadmap, wisdom and obedience are undeniably linked. Deuteronomy 4:5-6 says, *"See, I have taught you decrees and laws as the Lord my god commanded me, so that you may follow them in the land you are entering to take possession of it. Observe them carefully, for this will show your wisdom and understanding to the nations, who will hear about all these decrees and say, 'Surely this great nation is a wise and understanding people.'"*

Jesus is saying the same thing in the New Testament: *"Therefore everyone who hears these words of mine and puts them into practice is like a wise man who built his house on the rock,"* (Matthew 7:24). Godly wisdom doesn't include just reading and hearing, but also doing. You have to close the gap in your life between what you believe and how you behave. Obedience to God's Word breeds wisdom in our lives.

To be successful along this journey, you have to obey the Roadmap. There are certain things you just have to do to find your destination. If the GPS says, "Go right" and I go left, why would I be surprised that I missed where I was going? If God's Word says "Do this" or "Don't do that," why are we surprised when we miss our destination?

Quite often, people will quote a portion of John 8:32 that says, *"...you will know the truth, and the truth will set you free."* The verse before it is seldom quoted, *"Jesus said, 'If you hold to my teaching, you are really my disciples. Then...you will know the truth...."* Hold to His teaching. Be obedient to what His Word says and watch how the journey opens up before your eyes.

Let's Agree To Be Agreeable

There is something that is somewhat intangible, yet very powerful, when there is unanimity of opinion. The Bible talks about the power of agreement. *"Again, I tell you that if two of you on earth agree about anything you ask for, it will be done for you by my Father in heaven. For where two or three come together in my name, there am I with them,"* (Matthew 18:19-20). Many people read that passage, but they neglect what Jesus taught in His preceding words, *"I tell you the truth, whatever you bind on earth will be bound in heaven, and whatever you loose on earth will be loosed in heaven."*

Jesus is teaching those who would listen to Him that agreement is the key to releasing the power of God in our circumstances. It is saying to God, "I agree with You concerning what You are saying about my circumstances." It is through agreement with God that we can then move from the natural to the supernatural, from the ordinary to the extraordinary.

How important is the agreement of Christians and the unity of believers? Throughout the Bible, there are extraordinary exploits done when good people can put aside their agendas and link in to God's plan. Great military victories were won by Moses as Aaron and Hur came into agreement concerning the power of God to win a battle. David made a covenant with Jonathan that they both refused to break and God rewarded the nation of Israel. Jesus shared His ministry with His disciples and many miracles were displayed throughout the land. When Paul and Silas came into agreement in jail and began to sing in harmony, they found deliverance from their chains.

Is it any wonder why the Bible encourages us to come into agreement with each other? Just look through the New Testament some time and count how often we are told such things as:

> *"Love one another"* (John 13:34)
> *"Serve one another in love"* (Galatians 5:13)
> *"Be humble and gentle...bearing with one another"* (Ephesians 4:2)
> *"Forgive...one another"* (Colossians 3:13)
> *"Encourage each other"* (1 Thessalonians 4:18)
> *"Build each other up"* (1 Thessalonians 5:11)
> *"Spur one another"* (Hebrews 10:24)

Throughout the Bible, we are encouraged to come in agreement with God and each other. In fact, unity is commanded by Christ in John 13:34, *"A new command I give you: Love one another. As I have loved you, so you must love one another."* Jesus even prayed for us, *"...that all of them may be one. Father, just as you are in me and I am in you. May they also be in us so that the world may believe..."* (John 17:21). Agreement with what God says and who He is a prerequisite in understanding the journey that God has laid before you in this life. Not only that, and this may be more difficult: agreement with those around you can become a catalyst in your life.

No Matter What?

One of my favorite verses in the Bible is Jonah 3:1, *"Then the word of the Lord came to Jonah a second time."* Jonah had been disobedient when it came to God's destiny for his life. He deliberately ran from God's calling on His life and as a result, suffered significant consequences in his life. But, God came to Jonah and gave him a second chance. I am so grateful for second, third, and fourth chances when it comes to executing God's will for my life.

As many have said, failure isn't final unless you allow it. Jonah got up, cleaned himself up, and the second time, well, he got it right. As I mentioned earlier, I had tried to start a consulting firm with a couple of really close friends in 2006. It just didn't work. The good news is one of my friends has a great company as a result of the attempt. For me, it was the wrong time and wrong mission. God had carved out another time and mission for me. As a result, Sauls Consulting Services, Inc. now serves pastors and churches across America with great passion and excellence.

You may be very familiar with the Wesley brothers, John and Charles. However, you may not know the whole story. When they first met and heard General James Ogelthorpe, founder and governor of Georgia, speak about life in America with the natives and pioneers, they decided to go and bring the Gospel of Jesus Christ to the new land.

The result was, Charles who went as the governor's secretary, became very ill. John, who went to preach, fared even worse. The pioneers did not like his preaching or mannerisms, and the natives remained unconvinced no matter how hard he preached.

When the brothers returned to England, they should have been defeated and crushed by their overwhelming, highly publicized failures. Instead, it was apparent to all who knew them that their vision burned brighter than ever, though narrowed and sharpened by their experiences in America.

The God of the second chance turned the Wesleys' attention toward their homeland, England. At this time in history, the nation had drifted far from God and His leadership in their affairs. In fact, at this time in history, every sixth house in London had become a saloon. Drunkenness, child abandonment, bands of hooligans, and crime was everywhere. The church had grown ineffective and only functioned as a social club. It was chided by the upper class and ignored by the lower. Once again, the Wesley brothers seemed destined for failure. Their fiery preaching style was greeted with boos and jeers. They were pelted with stones, mud, and rotten eggs. However, something was different this time.

John literally leaped into his saddle, traveling throughout England, preaching up to five sermons a day for over fifty years. His message to the rich and poor was the same—"Repent and be saved!" He made faith in Christ a living reality. The nation was stirred by their efforts and the power of God at work. One of their converts, Robert Raikes, formed the first Sunday School, a movement that spread throughout the country and abroad. Society began to see the need to help abandoned children, the needy, illiterate and prisoners.

Not only did their message burn like wildfire throughout the nation of England, but also the message transcended the country and truly encircled the globe. Much of what is being done today in Christianity is a result of the fact that John and Charles Wesley, like Jonah, heard the Word of the Lord when it came a second time. Obedience, no matter what happens, can reshape your world and catapult you toward God's unique journey for your life.

Section 4

God's Intervention In The Journey

"That the Almighty does make use of human agencies and directly intervenes in human affairs is one of the plainest statements in the Bible. I have had so many evidences of His direction, so many instances when I have been controlled by some other power than my own will, that I cannot doubt that this power comes from above." - Abraham Lincoln

Chapter 11

Holy Discontentment That Leads To Holy Interventions

We live today in a culture that demands proof, truth, and evidence. We know terms like "truth in lending", "proof of purchase", and "full disclosure". Our government laws and regulations demand strict truth in lending facts, consumer statistics, ingredient lists, etc. We want to know what we are getting is what has been promised.

Is it any wonder the culture we live in demands the same thing from Christians? The term "hypocrite" is almost synonymous with Christians and church. Our nation hungers for something that is real, something that reflects a God of the Bible, a God of the miraculous. Our nation, and for that matter, the world, would love to see a God that resembles the Jesus of the Bible. They do not desire a sanitized, neatly packaged God that we so often get when we attend a church in America. People want to know that God is bigger than the issues and problems they are facing in our day. "If not, then why should I follow Him? If He cannot truly help me and change the circumstances I am living in, then why should I waste my time? There is enough little gods' around. I may as well chase after a dozen other entities that make claims, but never deliver."

Maybe you have heard some of those thoughts. Maybe you have thought some of those things. The Jesus of the Bible lived in the midst of the miracles during His three-year ministry on earth. The things He did could not have been done through human effort and power. If you can accept the Bible as truth and states historical accounts literally, then you would have to believe that Jesus functioned in an utter-worldly environment.

On one occasion, He spoke to a man by the name of Lazarus and this dead man came back to life. He would do things like spitting in the dirt and making a mud pie, then placing it on a guy's eyes and he would see. He performed many miracles like these, not in secret, but before friends, families, enemies, fault-finders, down-and-outers, and the elite alike. His works were such that those surrounding Him could not deny the facts. In fact, He freely welcomed examination of His miracles, although He never seemed to do them to draw attention to Himself.

One eyewitness of these miracles was the Apostle Peter, whom by trade was a fisherman. He left his profession to follow Jesus and in 2 Peter 1:16, he recounts, *"We did not follow cleverly invented stories when we told you about the power and coming of our Lord Jesus Christ, but we were eyewitnesses of his majesty."*

Before His ascension into heaven, Jesus went even a little further and sent out His followers with this miracle-filled mandate, *"I tell you the truth, anyone who has faith in me will do what I have been doing. He will do even greater things than these, because I am going to the Father,"* (John 14:12). There is a sense that Jesus actually expected us to function in the realm of the miraculous. If you have ever needed a miracle, it gets a lot easier to believe in them.

We have looked at a few mile markers that point us in the direction of becoming a fully committed follower of Jesus Christ. Capturing a vision for your life, resurrendering everything to Him, listening to His voice, and then walking out this journey in obedience, bring us to this marker. This mile marker is simply leaving room in your life for the miraculous to happen. God wants us to do what we can do, but then He wants us to leave room for Him.

This book was not written to convince you of the miraculous; I will leave that to people that are a lot smarter and more theologically educated than I am. There is a sense, in this chapter, that I have to assume you are among the convinced or at least willing to be convinced that, as Abraham Lincoln said, God "directly intervenes in human affairs." Everything does not have to fit neatly into our little categories of faith, because God can, and often does, come and do the unexplainable.

Once again, I do not know how all of it works. If I did, I would be as smart as God. And I'm not. But I do not have to explain it to believe it. I do not understand how some people receive miracles while others don't. God is God and He can do what He wants to do. And He does not have to ask my permission.

You can be a change agent for God. A life of ministering the miraculous most often begins with a holy discontentment for things as they are. The life and ministry of Jesus on this earth was committed to changing the status quo for all of eternity. When you look carefully at the history of the early church in the book of Acts, it is filled with men and women who became agents of change. What other reason would explain why the apostles were "flogged," told not to Go out and preach in that Name, and then immediately hit the streets preaching the death, burial, and resurrection of Jesus?

Could it be that God still wants to miraculously intervene in the lives of people in the twenty-first century? Have we become too sophisticated or "relevant" for God to show up and do the miraculous through people like you and me? He has called you and me to a "journey of the miraculous." He has called us to continue this miracle-filled legacy that extends throughout the Old and New Testament until today.

God wants to move you and me from what we think we can do to what He can do through us when we fully yield ourselves to Him. Our nation longs to see the miraculous. America is intrigued with spiritualism, miracles, and the unknown. I mean, just how many television shows can we get on with ghosts, ghosts sightings, the unknown beyond the grave, etc. So, why do we run so quickly as Christians from the misunderstood and unknown? Why do we find the miraculous so hard to embrace? A holy discontentment for where we currently are will drive us to a miraculous God who wants to intervene in our little worlds.

How Long Will We Waver?

> *"Elijah went before the people and said, 'How long will you waver between two opinions? If the Lord is God, follow Him, but if Baal is God, follow him,"* (1 Kings 24:21).

There is a story in the Old Testament of God's intervention for the nation of Israel. It takes place on Mount Carmel when the prophet, Elijah, openly threw down the challenge to four hundred fifty idol-worshiping prophets of Baal. He did so by simply asking the question, "Which one is the true God?" This was not a test for the weak of heart. This is the old school ground argument, "My dad is stronger than your dad. My dad can beat up your dad." Elijah wanted the people to see a concrete, unique demonstration of God's intervention and power.

Each side quickly agreed to make an altar of wood and stones with the meat of a bullock placed upon it. The worshipers of Baal prepared the bullock, placed it on the altar, called on the name of Baal from morning until past midday. They even leaped around the altar, cut themselves with knives, and cried loudly to heaven. Nothing, no response from their god.

Then it came for Elijah's test. He prepared an altar with twelve stones, one for each of the tribes of Israel. After the wood and the meat were in place, he did something that was very strange. He asked for four barrels of water to be poured over the sacrifice to prove further the power of the One and only True God. Then Elijah told the helpers to douse the sacrifice a second and third time with four more barrels of water each time. There was so much water that it ran all around the altar and filled the trench that encircled it.

Elijah then looked up to heaven and offered one of the most powerful prayers ever recorded in scripture: *"O Lord, God of Abraham, Isaac and Israel, let it be known today that you are God in Israel and that I am your servant and have done all these things at your command. Answer me, O Lord, answer me, so these people will know that you, O Lord, are God, and that you are turning their hearts back again,"* (1 Kings 18:36-37).

Elijah had a specific request and God gave a specific answer. *"Then the fire of the Lord fell and burned up the sacrifice, the wood, the stones and the soil, and also licked up the water in the trench. When all the people saw this, they fell prostrate and cried, 'The Lord—he is God! The Lord—he is God!"* (1 Kings 18:38-39).

Elijah was filled with a holy discontentment for the status of worship at that time. He could no longer take the idol worship that filled the nation. Today, a statue near Mount Carmel in Israel commemorates the victorious and divine intervention of the true God over the false prophets of Baal. Stories like this should embolden us today to believe God for the miraculous in the affairs of our nation. God desires courageous men and women to step forward and call out the false gods of our day.

Passing It On

> *"Elijah said to Elisha, 'Tell me, what can I do for you before I am taken from you?' 'Let me inherit a double portion of your spirit.' Elisha replied. 'You have asked a difficult thing,' Elijah said, 'yet if you see me when I am taken from you, it will be yours—otherwise not,'"* (2 Kings 2:9-10).

Some years later after the encounter with the false prophets of Baal, Elijah stumbled on to a man by the name of Elisha. He was plowing his field with a massive team of oxen, all one hundred twenty feet or so of beasts pulling the plow. At this moment, something happened so powerful that it would effect generations to come. The anointing on Elijah was so powerful that Elisha immediately slaughtered his oxen on the spot, held a massive tailgate party for all his neighbors, then followed Elijah and became his servant (1 Kings 19). There is very little said about Elisha during the remaining years of Elijah's life until the time when it became apparent that God was going to take Elijah into heaven in a whirlwind (2Kings 2).

After Elisha's double-portion anointing "ask," Elijah tested his commitment by asking him three times to remain while he went to Bethel, Jericho, and then over to Jordan. Elisha refused to leave the side of Elijah. Why? He did not want to be separated from the promised anointing. Elisha knew he would have to be in Elijah's presence when he was taken, so that meant being constantly by his side. There would be no anointing without action and obedience on his part. So, he kept moving, always close to Elijah, and then one day it happened, a chariot suddenly appears and Elijah went up to heaven in a whirlwind.

As Elijah's mantle fell, Elisha rushed to grab it and he caught the promised anointing: *"He picked up the cloak that had fallen from Elijah and went back and stood on the bank of the Jordan. Then he took the cloak that had fallen from him and struck the water with it. 'Where now is the Lord, the God of Elijah?' he asked. When he struck the water, it divided to the right and to the left, and he crossed over. The company of the prophets from Jericho, who were watching, said, 'The spirit of Elijah is resting on Elisha,'"* (2 Kings 2:13-15).

God arranges times when we are near the anointing, the miraculous, but if we hesitate or hold back, His touch will pass us by. Elisha had a holy discontentment with the way things were and refused to accept anything less than the double-portion anointing of God.

Many people want to receive great things from God. In fact, many desire to have the miraculous in their lives. However, few are willing to pay the price. We must be willing to stay close to His presence, cultivate intimacy with God, and get ready to receive what God has in store for us. May the cry of twenty-first century Christians be, "Lord, I hunger for a double portion of your anointing on my life. Let Your mantle fall on me!"

Chapter 12

Preparing For God's Intervention

"Miracles are a retelling in small letters of the very same story which is written across the world in letters too large for some of us to see." - C. S. Lewis

I am not the type of person who enjoys reminiscing in the past and living in yesteryear. That is just not my thing. I do not know nearly enough about my heritage, where my family came from, how we got here, and a lot of other family details that I should know. I live my life looking to the future and the possibilities that it holds.

I have never sat around thinking how wonderful it would have been to live during the time of Jesus and following Him around. I like comfort, and I do not think there was a lot of that going on during His time, at least, not for the Jewish people who were practically slaves to the Roman Empire. However, there are a couple of occasions in the New Testament that I wish I could have at least been a fly on the wall. One of those times was when Mary announced to her parents that she was pregnant by the Holy Spirit. Wouldn't you have loved to see her parents' faces? "Yeah, right, God got you pregnant! Who are you kidding?" That would have been a good one, although I'm sure her parents weren't feeling all that excited about he news. At least, not initially. I really do wonder how all that went down in their household that day.

There is another occasion that I think would have been quite fun to have had the opportunity to see the conclusion. That would be when the little boy came home after lending his lunch to Jesus and tried to explain to his mom how Jesus used it to feed thousands of people. "Son, I've told you about lying. I will not tolerate that in my house." That had to be a good conversation to spy on.

In the Bible, this story actually appears in all four gospels: Matthew, Mark, Luke, and John. Since it is the only miracle done by Jesus that appears in all four, I am guessing it must be pretty important. I also think there are some significant lessons we can take from this story. It is probably also the most famous of the miracles of Jesus because so many thousands of people saw it.

We know that Jesus never did a miracle to just show off; instead, He would do a miracle typically to teach a principle of the Kingdom of God. In this particularly story, Jesus is teaching us how to position ourselves to receive a miracle from God. Someday, you are going to need one if you don't need it right now. You may be thinking, *I could use a miracle right now in my life, in my family, in my finances, in my health, or in my relationships.*

So, how do I position myself for a miracle from God? Assuming God still does miracles, how can I get His attention? Miracles typically happen with a holy discontentment, a need, or a problem that is unsolvable by our human strength. If I can take care of it, then I do not need God to show up. But, if you are facing some things in your life that if God doesn't show up "you're in the tank," then you are probably in a position to see God do the miraculous in your life.

The good news is most of us have a need or a problem in our lives. If we don't have one right now, we will soon have one. So, read on! The story recorded in Mark 6, often referred to as The Feeding of the Five Thousand, did not begin with great faith. It did not begin because of prayer and fasting. This miracle began with needy people. In fact, every miracle Jesus performed during His early ministry began with a significant need or problem. In this particular story, there is this growing multitude of people that have been following Jesus for days. They had been listening to Him teach, do miracles, bring deliverances, and now, it is the end of the day. Everyone is tired, thousands need to be fed, and there is no Chick-fil-A around. There is a problem and it is not going to get fixed by human effort or ingenuity.

For God to work in our lives, we need to be totally honest with Him and confess that we have a need bigger than us. God does not work in my life until I ask Him to work in my life. This is a difficult thing for many people because we would rather go on in denial than to admit, "I need God to show up." We live in a very self-sufficient culture that says, "I can do it, I will make it happen!" That attitude is a powerful deterrent to God doing the miraculous. It doesn't mean He can't—He just won't!

This story lets us know that it was near the end of the day and the people were hungry. They had this problem all day and they could see the inevitable coming, but they didn't do anything about it. Have you ever done that? Have you ever faced what looked like an impossible situation and you just said, "Why do today what I can do tomorrow?" Maybe it was your children, finances, marriage, or career. And all he did, ignoring of the problem, was increase the pressure.

There is a saying I have heard that goes like this: "People do not change until the pain they are living in becomes greater than the pain of change." Certainly, ignoring the problem or not taking responsibility for it will not make it go away. Even the disciples in this story said to Jesus, *"Send them away."* Worrying about it won't change it, either. The disciples began to worry rather than recognizing that God was there with them. The very One that spoke the world into existence was in their midst. They were looking to the wrong source for the solution.

We do the very same thing. We tend to look everywhere but at God. We forget that He is referred to in the Bible as Emmanuel. God is with us. You just cannot forget that He is with you.

Not only do we need to admit to God that we have a need, but we have to personally get involved in the process. We tend to stand back and cheer God, but we don't want to get involved. As my good friend, Steve Robinson, says, "Oftentimes, what we are looking for from God is not a miracle, but magic." However, one of the lessons we can learn from this passage is that God wants us to be involved with what He is doing in this world. In this story, the little boy surrendered his lunch of fish and bread and the disciples got involved by distributing the food to the thousands as Jesus multiplied the little boy's lunch. Jesus tells the disciples in Mark 6:37a, *"You give them something to eat."*

Jesus had them to access what they had in verse 38, *"How many loaves do you have. Go and see. When they found out, they said, 'five—and two fishes."* When God intervenes in our lives, he starts with what we have. You do not have to concern yourself with what you do not have. God is saying to you, "What do you have in your hands? Let's start with that."

God wants your involvement in your life and in the lives of those around you who need a miracle. But it is hard to get our attention and our involvement when we are comfortable. The little boy didn't need a miracle that day. He had food. He was the only one that did not need the miraculous and God used him as the catalyst for the miraculous.

God starts with our talent, energy, abilities, gifts, resources, experiences, faith, etc., and He waits to see what we are going to do with what we have before He intervenes from the world of the supernatural. God knows the need before you do. He is never surprised by what surprises us. But He often waits to see what we will do with what we have. Will we participate in the supernatural along with Him?

Has God ever asked you to participate with Him in the miraculous, but it just did not make sense? Think about the thousands and thousands of people on the hillside that particular day versus one bag lunch. It did not make sense to His disciples. However, faith in God says we give because God requires it, not because it makes sense. God does not just look at my bank account, or my education, or my abilities; God is looking at my faith, obedience, and willingness to get involved with Him.

Psalms 24:1 reminds us that everything belongs to God and so we should never have any problem putting it back in His hands, *"The earth is the Lord's, and everything in it, the world, and all who live in it."* All we can hope to do is return to the Lord what is already His. You cannot give what is not yours. All we can do is participate with God in the miraculous by giving Him everything He has given to us. It is not that He needs it; it is His. God loves it when we give to Him willingly. He loves the attitude of willingness. God loves it when we give to Him immediately upon Him asking. Delayed obedience is disobedience. And God loves it when we give to Him cheerfully. An attitude of gratitude is a tremendous spark for the miraculous.

To see the miraculous, your faith will have to allow you to believe in expectation. Nothing seems to happen in the Kingdom of God until we expect it to happen. In Mark 6:42, it says, *"They all ate and were satisfied..."*.

What do you need more of in your life? Time? That may mean you need to give more of your time away. Money? You may need to give more generously. Whatever you give to God, He will take it, multiply it, and bless it in return to you.

God has set a principle in life called the principle of sowing and reaping. You may have heard it referred to as the Law of Reciprocity. Whatever you are willing to sow or give away, you are going to reap. If you give away encouragement, you will reap encouragement. If you give away criticism, guess what? You know! God has set this in order and every good farmer knows it's true.

By the way, you never reap or harvest in the same season you sow. You sow in one season and you reap in another. So, do not become impatient with God.

Early on in this story recorded in Mark 6, the disciples had come to Jesus and asked Him, *"Lord, there's thousands of hungry people. What are You going to do?"* And Jesus just looks at them and says, *"Hey, you feed them. You give them something to eat."* Jesus was asking the impossible, both physically and financially. In John 6:6, it is the same story, and it says, *"He asked this only to test them, for he already had in mind what he was going to do."* He was testing that faith and obedience. You do not get very far in the journey without faith that God is and will do what He says He will do. And, being obedient to what He calls you to do or ask you to do.

God already has in mind what He is going to do about the needs in your life. This season may be a test. Are you going to give Him what you already have in your hands? There are three levels of giving for you and what God has entrusted to you. You can give to God at a level that you can afford. Basically, you are giving without giving anything up. That is the lowest level of giving. Alternatively, you could give by giving something up. This is still measured in the natural realm because you can see it and it is logical in your thinking. Or you can choose to trust God to give through you. What if I choose to behave in a sacrificial manner and trust God to be my source? What if I measured my life not by what I can give because then I am the source? But what if I measured my life by what God can give through me? That is participating in the miraculous. God becomes the source, not me.

What would happen if you allowed God to work through you? What would happen in your life if you allowed God to give through you? I spoke in a church in St. Petersburg, Russia, in 1995. This was not too long after the Berlin Wall came down. Russia was experimenting with capitalism and an open culture. This church met in a movie theater and they allowed them to have lights, but no heat. And they had to be out by noon so they could prepare for the matinee movie crowd.

As I spoke that morning on a miracle from the Old Testament, I noticed these Russian ladies in the front rows weeping. I was thinking to myself, *I can't be that bad*. After I had finished, I asked the translator what was going on with those ladies near the front. She went over and spoke to them briefly and came back. This was what she said to me that day: "Those ladies were crying because they were happy and mad. They were mad because they had been lied to for seventy years and did not know about miracles. They were happy because they now know that this God they are getting to know is a God of the miraculous."

He is a God of the miraculous and He desires to work in your life. Will you cooperate with Him? Do not let anyone lie to you or talk you out of the miraculous. God is still at work in this world and He wants to supernaturally work in and through you.

Saint Augustine said, "Miracles are not contrary to nature, but only contrary to what we know about nature." Get honest with God and admit you need His intervention in your life. When you see something in our world that creates holy discontentment inside of you, pray that God will move and do the miraculous in that situation. Prepare for a miracle. Expect God's divine intervention. It will catapult you down the journey that God has designed specifically for you.

Chapter 13

The Intervention On The Journey

Most everyone knows what it is like to have your day interrupted by something unforeseen. I have a great program on my iPad that I use for planning called "ToDo." I typically sit down in my office at the beginning of the month and plan out my travel schedule for the month. The idea is to make all the arrangements for travel and plan my month as to get the best prices for travel expense. I do the same thing again at the beginning of each week. I plan out my week to balance my writing, management of Sauls Consulting, travel schedule, and personal time. Then, at the conclusion of each day, I plot out the work for the next day.

I know all this sounds a little laborious and meticulous but with someone who is very close to ADD, it is critical that I have this kind of organization in my life. It certainly does not come naturally, so it is a little painful to sit down and try to be organized. With my very best efforts, it is not unusual to have my daily, weekly, and monthly plans interrupted frequently. Sometimes, the interruptions are "God interventions" and in a few moments the shape of my day, in fact, some times my life is radically changed. God's interventions are those moments, times, or events when that which is supernatural invades the natural.

For a moment, consider this event in the life of Apostle Paul before he became Paul, as recorded in Acts 9:1-6. *"Meanwhile, Sauls was still breathing out murderous threats against the Lord's disciples. He went to the high priest and asked him for letters to the synagogues in Damascus, so that if he found any there who belonged to the Way, whether men or women, he might take them as prisoners to Jerusalem. As he neared Damascus on his journey, suddenly a light from heaven flashed around him. He fell to the ground and heard a voice say to him, 'Saul, Saul, why do you persecute me?' 'Who are you, Lord?' Sauls asked. 'I am Jesus, whom you are persecuting,' he replied. 'Now get up and go into the city, and you will be told what you must do.'"*

Saul, before he became Paul, was on a clear-cut mission to destroy Christianity. He had received authority from the high priest (likely Caiaphas) to represent the Sanhedrin in persecuting Christians throughout the region. That was the agenda and his purpose for traveling to Damascus. But, God intervened! However, God in this moment changed the agenda of Saul's life completely.

When you read those verses, one of the things you have to notice is that Paul did not fall into a theological debate with this mystery voice that he all of a sudden interrupted his life. He simply asked, *"Who are you, Lord?"* And the answer, *"I am Jesus,"* was enough to impact the history of the world for all of eternity. What may have even initially seen by Saul as a higher power trying to get his attention, would be seen as him transitioning from leadership in Jewish society to being used to turn the world upside down with the gospel of Jesus Christ. He did not know that he would be used by the Holy Spirit to pen most of the New Testament. He did not know that he would be used to take the gospel to most of the known world at that time. He did not know that he would be used to confront leaders and whole nations with the person of Jesus Christ. What he did know was God had miraculously intervened in his life and his world would never be the same. His obedience to what he did not understand on that road to Damascus is an incredible example of how we are to respond to God's interventions in our lives.

In one moment of the miraculous, God took Saul, a persecutor of His church, and made him the Apostle Paul, a chosen vessel of God's intervention into this world. In fact, later in this story, God speaks to Ananias and tells him to go and minister to the blinded Saul. *"Go! This man is my chosen instrument to carry my name before the Gentiles and their kings and before the people of Israel,"* (Acts 9:15).

Our daily interventions from God may not be as dramatic and life changing as Paul's, but we are called to a journey that could change the course of our lives at any moment. The miraculous is the miraculous! It's unpredictable! You cannot harness it for a predictable occasion. Daniel 11:32 says, *"The people who know their God shall be strong, and carry out great exploits."* A willingness to open our heart to God's intervention is fundamental to seeing the miraculous occur in our lives.

Intervention In Your Family

God has uniquely promised Christians that He is concerned for our families and He will "contend" or fight on our behalf for our family. Isaiah 49:25 says, *"I will contend with those who contend with you, and your children I will save."* I have found great comfort in those words, having two sons who have just completed their teenage years. They are now both in college and I still hold on to those words every single day of my life. I understand the responsibility I have as a parent and their responsibility in leading their lives, but it has brought great comfort to many parents just to know that God does supernaturally intervene in the journey of our children.

My boys were raised as PK's. If you do not get the Christianese involved with those letters, it means "Pastor's Kids." They will tell you that they enjoyed every single day of being the sons of the pastor. We were very careful to protect our children from the politics and "inside stories" of the church I pastored; therefore, to this day, our boys love God, His people, and the institution of the church. Listen, I am not saying they are perfect little soldiers for God. But, they are among a group of grown PK's who have a tremendous respect for the Kingdom of God. Sometimes, I think that may be a miracle by itself. At times, Christians can lose sight of the big picture. They can be very difficult on pastors, and maybe sometimes we deserve it.

I am so grateful that I have always sensed the supernatural going on around my boys and the hand of God on their lives. I know every parent feels their children are the best and God especially smiled on them. Guess what? I feel the same way. My wife and I had been trying to have children for about five years with no luck. After nine years of marriage and about five years of trying to conceive, she walked into my office one day at church and announced, "I'm pregnant!" Say what you want, but I believe God supernaturally intervened and gave us David. We had tried numbers of methods to have a child and nothing worked. At a point when we were not trying anything and really not thinking about it, she got pregnant. I am just going to say it: That's God!

Three and a half years later, Jonathan came along. Having another child was not even on our radar screen. Yet, God intervened again and blessed us with another son. Both of my sons have accepted Christ and I had the privilege of baptizing them while I was their pastor. Let's look at some of what the Bible has to say about God's intervention in your family as you are moving on this journey

Family is God's idea. He established the family with Adam and Eve from the very beginning of human history. *"So God created man in his own image, in the image of God he created him; male and female he created them. God blessed them and said to them, 'Be fruitful and increase in number,'"* (Genesis 1:27-28). In other words, go have some kids. Get at it! And they did. And the human race, with the blessing of family, was off and running.

A few chapters later in the Bible, God confirms His feelings for family. Genesis 7:1 declares, *"The Lord then said to Noah,*

'Go into the ark, you and your whole family, because I have found you righteous in this generation.'" We know the story from there. Noah's entire family was saved from the flood that came upon the earth. God desires to preserve your family and save them from the craziness that often surrounds us in this life.

Let's advance forward in human history to the story of the first Passover when the Israelites were being held in captivity in Egypt. *"Each man is to take a lamb for his family, one for each household,"* (Exodus 12:3). It was the shed blood of each household's lamb that would cover the family and spare the children from death. It is the shed blood of our Savior that has covered our children and spares them from the assaults of the Evil One who desires to "kill, steal, and destroy." That was the supernatural intervention of God in the journey of God's children in the Old Testament.

I am sure you have had days were you just had to step back and say words very similar to those that Joshua declared over his family, *"But if serving the Lord seems undesirable to you, then choose for yourselves this day whom you will serve, whether the gods your forefathers served beyond the River, or the gods of the Amorites, in whose land you are living. But as for me and my household, we will serve the Lord,"* (Joshua 24:15). Joshua makes a clear declaration that this thing is not just about him, but his whole family. What is it that you are speaking over your family these days? As one television host says, "What say you?"

If we go over to the New Testament, we will see the same thing represented in scripture. God wants to intervene supernaturally in the life of your family. Look at these words in Acts 16:14-15 as it shares the story of a new believer in Christ named Lydia, *"The Lord opened her heart to respond to Paul's message...she and the members of her household were baptized."* And there are other examples in the history of the early church where whole families were swept into the Kingdom of God. In fact, a little later in that same chapter, there is the story of a Philippian jailer, who not only became a new believer, but his whole family received the miracle of salvation.

You can see a principle of God's intervention in the family all throughout scripture. So, why shouldn't we believe the same thing about our family that God believes? He believes in you and every member of your family. Salvation has been provided for your family and right now would be a great time to declare that fact over your family if you haven't already.

Obviously, we know that each person in our family has a free choice to make about what he or she will do with Jesus. Ultimately, each is responsible to God for the decision to accept or reject His plan for his or her eternal destiny, but we can play a key role in God's plan by praying for our children and believing that God will draw them to Himself.

While pastoring in North Carolina, I saw how one young man came to Christ. Not too long after that, his mother received salvation. In a matter of weeks, his sister, brother-in-law, and nephews all received Christ in their lives. It started with one young man who prayed and God swept his whole family into the Kingdom.

I have a great family heritage and both of my parents have served the Lord all of my life. I cannot remember a time growing up when church was not the center of our family life. I don't know my dad's family very well. He was the next to youngest of sixteen children, so his mom and dad had passed away before I was born. Probably from exhaustion! I do know quite a bit more about my mom's family.

As a little guy, I remember going to my grandparent's house and it was the joy of my young life. I loved my grandparents and my granddad seemed bigger than life to me. My mom is the oldest of the children and she has five brothers. All six of my grandparent's children are Christians and not only that, they serve the Lord with all their hearts. I am the oldest of thirteen grandchildren, all boys by the way. We could play whatever sport was in season when we got together. There were plenty of boys to get it done.

One of my cousins, Terry, passed away a few years ago. But here's what I do know: all of us serve the Lord. This is the miracle of salvation that has covered generations of the Smith's. As a footnote to this story, my granddad was not a Christian during the years I was growing up. In the latter part of his life, he went to a public altar at a church as his oldest son was preaching, and received Christ as his Savior. Just one more thought and I will be quiet on the legacy of my family. My grandmother's mom was also a very devoted Christian that even in the latter part of her 70s, she went to Israel on a Holy Land Tour. Unfortunately, she did not get to finish the tour. She actually broke her hip walking down to the edge of the Jordan River. What a beautiful, generational heritage I have as a Christian.

I see this even in my brother, Tony's, life today. His whole family serves the Lord and their lives are filled with church activities. Tony and his wife, Stephanie, are very active in their small group. In other words, God and his people are at the center of their life.

Family is God's big idea and He loves your family more than you do. He has a plan for you and everyone that is a part of your household. He has set aside a unique spiritual journey for all of us and God desires to intervene supernaturally in that journey from time to time.

The spiritual journey set aside by God for you personally can be filled with moments of the miraculous. In fact, how boring would the journey be if we lived our lives so safely and without faith moments that God didn't have to show up. I love living my life out in faith territory. It is the kind of life where God is constantly showing up and bailing me out. The upside is simply God is always showing up in my life. I have chosen to live my life invaded by God moments. And, you can, too!

EPILOGUE

So, What's The Promise?

During the early years of my college education, in my heart I wanted to be the next John Lennon of Beatles fame. My dream was to become a rock star, write great songs, and perform before thousands of screaming fans. Needless to say, that dream never materialized. Anyway, you cannot live someone else's dream. That one has already been done.

In those college days, I loved Christian music like Andrae Crouch and some of the more contemporary musicians of the 70s, but I did not like church music. In fact, in the last year, I sent Andrae a note on Facebook, although I'm sure he has never seen it. Essentially, I told him I think he probably saved my life. I would often think of Christian music and just say to myself, "If I have to listen to one more Blackwood Brothers or Happy Goodman song, I'm going to cut my wrist." Now, I'm sure it really wasn't that bad, but for a teenager, I just did not feel it spoke to me or had any relevance to my life. "There's going to be a big homecoming in the sky" just was not speaking to me spiritually or musically.

I wanted to play rock and roll and I liked Lennon. His style, sound, rebellion, everything about him was where I wanted to be. As my parents know now, I would sneak around on weekends and play with rock bands, but I would always be back for church on Sunday morning ready to sing in the church, play the trumpet, or drums, or piano, or guitar, or whatever they needed me to do. I loved the Lord and never hated going to church, but my heart was in rock and roll.

During my sophomore year in college, God truly began to work in my life through various people, but one of the most influential was Jeff Gibson. Jeff was an outstanding musician, loved the Lord, and played contemporary Christian music. Beyond everything, Jeff was a fully committed follower of Jesus Christ. His influence in my life led me to be more open to the voice of God and what He might be saying to me about my life journey. God finally had my full attention and I later transferred to a small Christian college and pursued God's call to ministry for my life.

When I look back over my journey, I truly can see the fingerprints of God all over my life. I believe He has always been there at every turn in the path and has gently led me even when I did not want to go where He was taking me. In fact, I sometimes did not go where He was taking me.

Here's the truth that I do not want to escape you as you move along in the journey that God has laid out for you. There is a promise that is recorded in the Bible that says, *"I will never leave you or forsake you."* I know you probably have heard that verse and read it a million times, but my hope is that you will own it personally in your life.

There have been times in my life that I did not feel Him or necessarily believed that He cared about my journey. However, when I look back through the rearview mirror of my life, I can see His hand all over the place. I hold on to The Promise. I have to believe that God is continuously shaping and working in my life. Although I may not see or feel Him actively at work in my life, He is always there.

I have had some significant game changing crossroads in my life and it is the confidence that I find by looking back at them that gives me the courage to face the crossroads in front of me at this point in the journey. You cannot live your life looking in the rearview mirror because eventually, you will crash. Nevertheless, you have to glance up occasionally to see where you have been because it gives you courage to continue. It is The Promise. God is with us. God is with you and He will never leave or forsake you.

If you have not experienced God's presence in the everyday journey of your life, it will be more difficult for you to experience His presence in those "crossroads moments" that are inevitable in your life. It is not a matter of "if," but when you will come to the next crossroad. God designed these "crossroads moments" in our lives as a catalyst to move us exponentially forward in the journey He has designed for us. Your attitude toward these moments will determine if they knock you off the path or move you forward with new hope and faith that God is who He says He is and He will do what He says He will do. Oh, and by the way, God is God, so He doesn't have to ask our permission. He created you in His image and He is still creating "crossroads moments" in your life that truly shape your path.

To prepare you for those inevitable moments, start now. Don't wait until you get in the moment. It will be too late. Develop a vision statement that will guide you through this journey. Keep it simple and always remember that God is with you. It is The Promise. Make it simple, keep it short, and make it personal. Don't try to steal someone else's journey. God uniquely made you, called you, and equipped you for the journey He created for you. Get it! I hope you got it!

Remember that vision will help you to say "Yes" to the right things in the journey and "No" to the wrong things. It provides boundaries and margin for your life. Otherwise, the clutter of the life journey will get your attention and what is important will get buried. You wake up twenty years later and wonder what happened to your life. Allow the vision to be the roadmap and remember The Promise. God is with you. He will never leave or forsake you.

As you work through your vision statement, go ahead and resurrender everything to God. Once again, make sure that every facet of your life is on the altar and that you clearly understand that it is your responsibility to manage your life, but God owns it. He created you, and He who creates, owns! It does not mean that you have no responsibilities. Conversely, it means you have a lot of responsibility.

The more gifted God has made you, the more responsibility you have for redeeming that which He has invested in you. This is truly the great stewardship question of life. What are you doing with what God has given to you? Have you surrendered it to Him? Have you taken the time to inventory your life and see if there are areas that need to be resurrendered to Him?

Don't live your life the way so many Americans have chosen to live. We are a nation committed to one thing: not committing. We live our journey as though we are in a buffet line at a great cafeteria. We keep walking down the line and we see so many things we like, but we want to keep our options open. All of a sudden, we are at the end of the buffet and we have nothing on our plate. Too many people live their lives wanting to keep their options open just in case something better comes along. Then they get down to the end of life and they have done nothing with what God has given to them.

Manage well and the rewards will be great. Allow Him to shape your journey and use the gifts, abilities, personality, talents, resources, family, and experiences He has graciously provided to you. And remember The Promise. As you steward your life well, He will be with you. No matter how many times you make mistakes or take things off the altar of resurrender, He will be right there. It is a Promise.

Hearing the voice of God and discerning it well will keep you out of a lot of ditches along the journey. He is always speaking; are you always listening? How God speaks to you is uniquely different from how He speaks to anyone else. God is a creative God. Don't try to put Him in a box and think He only communicates one way. He is far too creative to be marginalized in that manner.

Sometimes, it's a whisper and you recognize Him because you have spent time with Him. Recognition is based on familiarity. If you never communicate with Him, you will not recognize His voice. As mentioned earlier, He is always speaking; are you always listening? Often, he communicates to you through His Word. You read a passage that you have read a hundred times, but this time it jumps off the page. God is speaking to you through His Word. As you are reading His Word today, remember The Promise. He is with you as you are reading. Why would He not want to speak to you?

Now, here is the catch: when He speaks to you, do you respond in obedience? It is one thing to hear God's voice, it is another to be obedient to His voice. It is not always the easiest or most convenient thing to do. Remember when God spoke to Abraham and told him to leave his homeland. It was with no explanation of where he was going that Abraham uprooted his whole family and started on the journey. He didn't tell him where, how long, what it would cost, or when he was coming back. Abraham understood The Promise. The only thing he knew about the journey was the most important element. God was with him and his family. Everything else paled in comparison to that one truth. The Promise!

Last, leave room for God's miraculous intervention in your journey. Stay close to Him so when you come to those "crossroads moments," you know The Promise. You have full confidence that God is going to intervene and use your life and resources to advance His kingdom. God wants to get incredible resources into your life. Our responsibility is to steward them well and make ourselves available for "miracle moments." Can God trust you with the bigger things in life? Have you been faithful in the small moments? God will use you for great exploits if you are prepared for those moments.

Through the first sixteen years of my sons' lives, I allowed them to use small things around the home. It was not a huge step for me to trust them with my car when they turned sixteen. Why? Because they had been responsible in the smaller moments. Our Heavenly Father, who is a Perfect Father, does the same thing in our lives. The small moments prepare us for the huge moments He has prepared for us. How are you doing in preparation for the big crossroad moment?

Enjoy the journey! No two days are alike. No two paths are alike. Enjoy the uniqueness of the journey God has prepared for you. As I have often heard it said, we are fellow sojourners in this world. Let's not be jealous of another person's journey. Instead, let's cheer each other on. And always remember: never forget The Promise. You don't do The Journey alone. *"I will never leave you, nor forsake you."*

Travel wisely!

ABOUT SAULS CONSULTING SERVICES, INC.

Sauls Consulting Services, Inc. was founded in 2007 by Dr. Glenn Sauls. SCS is a comprehensive church consulting firm providing partnerships to local churches and pastors in the areas of capital stewardship campaigns, annual stewardship campaigns, pastoral / staff coaching, and networking with church loan organizations, church architectural firms, and church contractors. Our organization has long experience in providing churches with outstanding consultation in the arena of stewardship campaigns that engages all the ministry areas. The comprehensive strategy implemented by SCS allows the local church to remain focused on ministry while raising the necessary funding for ministry and/or facility expansion. It also provides a strong format for sustainable and maximum results in the areas of spiritual and financial development.

For more information, you can go to the SCS website at www.SaulsConsulting.com.

CPSIA information can be obtained at www.ICGtesting.com
Printed in the USA
LVOW082025151211

259659LV00001B/2/P